AF600626

THE CATHOLIC UNIVERSITY OF AMERICA
Canon Law Studies
No. 317

THE POWER OF THE LOCAL ORDINARY TO IMPOSE A MATRIMONIAL BAN

A HISTORICAL SYNOPSIS AND A COMMENTARY

by

REV. JOHN M. WATERHOUSE, J. C. L.
Priest of the Diocese of Ogdensburg

A DISSERTATION

Submitted to the Faculty of the School of Canon Law of the Catholic University of America in Partial Fulfillment of the Requirements for the Degree of Doctor of Canon Law

THE CATHOLIC UNIVERSITY OF AMERICA PRESS
WASHINGTON, D. C.
1952

Nihil obstat:

JOANNES ROGG SCHMIDT, J. C. D.

Censor Deputatus

Washingtonii, D. C., die 30 aprilis 1950

Imprimatur:

✠ BRYAN J. MCENTEGART, D. D., LL. D.

Episcopus Ogdensburgensis

Ogdensburgi, die 25 martii 1952

PRINTED IN THE UNITED STATES OF AMERICA
BY ST. ANTHONY GUILD PRESS, PATERSON, N. J.

TO

HIS EXCELLENCY

THE MOST REVEREND BRYAN J. McENTEGART, D. D., LL. D.

Bishop of Ogdensburg

TABLE OF CONTENTS

FOREWORD

The Church is ever a vigilant custodian of the sanctity of matrimony, and takes all possible precautions that nothing shall impede or nullify the proposed marriage contract. Therefore, whenever there exists a probable doubt concerning the possibility of contracting an invalid, illicit, or inadvisable union, it has provided that the persons concerned be forbidden to proceed with the intended marriage ceremony until an investigation has revealed the presence or absence of an impediment, or until the condition which renders the marriage inadvisable has been removed. This process of temporarily forbidding a marriage is known as the imposition of a personal ban. The power to impose this matrimonial ban in particular instances for a just cause is granted to all local ordinaries by canon 1039, §1, of the Code of Canon Law.

The writer takes this occasion to express his gratitude to His Excellency, the Most Reverend Bryan J. McEntegart, D. D., LL. D., Bishop of Ogdensburg, for the opportunity to pursue advanced studies in Canon Law; to the members of the faculty of the School of Canon Law, The Catholic University of America, for their guidance and assistance in the preparation of this work; to his fellow students and all the others who made his course of study at the university valuable as well as pleasant.

PART ONE

HISTORICAL SYNOPSIS

CHAPTER I

NATURE AND ORIGIN OF THE IMPEDIMENT OF PERSONAL BAN

In general there are two kinds of impediments to marriage — impedient and diriment. The impedient impediments are those which are imposed by the Church in such a way that when they exist, the faithful are forbidden to marry; however, if they do marry in spite of this prohibition, the marriage is valid. On the other hand, the diriment impediments are those which are imposed by the Church in such a way that, when they exist, the faithful are forbidden to marry under penalty of invalidity of the marriage, for they prevent the existence of the contract.[1]

A personal ban issued by the Church originally was one of the impedient impediments. This simply implied the forbidding of a certain specified marriage by the Church or by an ecclesiastical judge.[2]

Although a marriage contracted in the face of any of the impedient impediments can be said to be contracted against the prohibition of the Church — inasmuch as the Church forbids the contracting of marriage in the face of these impediments — nevertheless, a personal ban at one time constituted a special impediment, distinct from the others, inasmuch as it was imposed by the Church or by an ecclesiastical judge on persons who were not bound by any of the other impediments. For ecclesiastical judges in all times had cases every now and then which required them to prohibit marriage to certain persons for a time, even though there existed no specified impediment.[3]

St. Thomas (1225-1274) placed this impediment in his list of impedient impediments. In his writings on the *Fourth Book of the Sentences* he stated: "Marriage can be prohibited in a twofold manner. In one way, it can be through something which is contrary to the solemnity of the sacrament; and such impediments exist as a hindrance

1. Theodorus M. Rupprecht, *Notae Historicae in Universum Ius Canonicum* (Venetiis, 1764), Lib. IV, tit. I et unicus, *de sponsalibus et matrimonio,* Par. VI, p. 381, n. 86.

2. *Loc. cit.*

3. *Loc. cit.*

for the contracting agent, but they do not invalidate the agent's contract. They are two: the prohibition of the Church and the forbidden periods."[4]

Sylvester Prierias (Mazolinus Sabaudus) (1456-1523) centuries later stated the same thing in slightly different language: "Certain impediments prohibit the contracting of marriage, but do not dissolve the contract, inasmuch as they make it impossible to contract such a marriage without sin. If, however, such a marriage is contracted, it stands — as is the case with the impediment of a personal ban issued by the Church."[5]

According to Petrus de Palude (1270-1342), a marriage could stand contrary to the prohibition of the Church in a twofold manner: first, inasmuch as it stood contrary to a statute of law in that the latter forbade the contracting of marriage at some given time or in some specific way (v. g., in a clandestine manner); and, secondly, inasmuch as it stood contrary to a personal ban, that is, to a precept which someone as an agent of the law and of the Church issued with a legitimate reason for the purpose of barring the celebration of some specific marriage.[6]

Bernard of Pavia († 1213) made the point that the Church's prohibition of the contracting of a marriage could be considered in either of two meanings. In a wide or general acceptation it related

---

4. *Sancti Thomae Aquinatis Doctoris Angelici Opera Omnia,* Tomus XXII (Parmae, 1868), *Opuscula Alia Dubia,* Vol. I, complectens *Scriptum in IV Libros Magistri Sententiarum et Opusculum de Praescientia et Praedestinatione,* Lib. IV, Distinctio XXXIV et XXXV, Quaestio Unica, art. 1: "Respondeo. Dicendum quod matrimonium impediri potest dupliciter. Uno modo, per aliquid quod contrariatur sacramenti solemnitati; et hujusmodi impedimenta impediunt contrahendum, sed non dirimunt contractum: et sunt duo, idest prohibitio Ecclesiae et tempus feriatum. Unde versus: Ecclesiae vetitum, nec non tempus feriatum impediunt fieri, permittunt juncta teneri." (Translation by the author.)

5. "Quaedam impedimenta impediunt matrimonium contrahendum, sed non dirimunt contractum, in quantum scilicet faciunt ut contrahi non possit sine peccato. Si tamen contrahat, de facto tenet, sicut interdictum ecclesiae." — *Summa Sylvestrina, Quae Summa Summorum merito Nuncupatur* (2 vols., Venetiis, 1601), Pars Secunda, *Matrimonium,* VI, p. 146, n. 2 (hereafter cited *Summa Sylvestrina*). (Translation by the author.)

6. *Ibid.,* p. 147, n. 1.

to any marriage contracted contrary to the prescriptions of Canon Law. Especially was this true when the marriage was attempted in violation of a law that established a diriment impediment. In another and a more restricted sense, however, the prohibition implied a legitimate superior's temporary precept through which a particular couple was forbidden to contract marriage.[7] It was in the latter acceptation that this matrimonial impediment could be defined as a special and particular preceptive prohibition of a competent ecclesiastical superior, temporarily imposed in view of some legitimate and just cause, and generally with the effect that it became illicit for the couple to contract the prohibited marriage.[8]

Although in canonical legislation one and the same term was employed to designate both the ecclesiastical penalty of interdict and the matrimonial impediment, nevertheless these two were not to be identified. The penalty of interdict was inflicted subsequent to the perpetration of some delict, whereas the matrimonial impediment of the same name was imposed previous to the commission of a delict and with the express purpose of preventing an invalid, illicit, or temporarily inadvisable marriage, and of thereby precluding the imposition of specific penalties.

In the early centuries of the Church there was no official mention of the canonical institute here under consideration, nor were there any canons dealing expressly with the Church's prohibition of marriage by way of a personal ban. However, it cannot be said there were no traces of it whatsoever. From the very beginning there were certain elementary indications of the innate and proper right of the Church to establish impediments, either by law or by precept — certain vague foreshadowings presaging the later development of the concept of this impediment.

7. Bernardus Papiensis, *Summa Decretalium* (ed. E. Laspeyres, Ratisbonae, 1860), tit. *de matrimonio contra interdictum ecclesiae contracto* (IV, 17), p. 2, n. 1: "... non consulendo, sed jubendo."

8. Henricus Cardinalis Hostiensis (Henricus de Segusio), *Summa Aurea* (Venetiis, 1586), tit. *de matrimonio contra interdictum ecclesiae contracto,* p. 317, n. 2.

For instance, in the very infancy of the Church, St. Ignatius the Martyr († 107) instructed the first Christians that they should enter marriage only with the sanction of their bishop.[9]

Some centuries later, in the year 633, the IV Provincial Council of Toledo forbade clerics of inferior rank to enter certain marriages without the permission of their bishop.[10]

But the first example of a pontifical prohibition is not found until the year 770. At that time Stephen IV (768-772) forbade Charlemagne, under penalty of anathema and invalidity of the marriage, to marry the daughter of the Longobard king, or to allow his sister to marry the brother of the Longobard king.[11]

A century later John VIII (872-882) forbade a certain widow to contract marriage with a foreigner. In fact, he required her either

---

9. "For those of both sexes who contemplate marriage it is proper to enter the union with the sanction of the bishop." — *Ancient Christian Writers, The Works of the Fathers in Translation,* edited by Johannes Quasten and Joseph C. Plumpe, Vol. I, *The Epistles of St. Clement of Rome, and St. Ignatius of Antioch,* newly translated and annotated by James A. Kleist, S. J. (Westminster, Maryland: The Newman Bookshop, 1946), "Letter of Ignatius to Polycarp," p. 98, n. 5.

10. Can. 44: "Clerici qui sine consultu episcopi sui aut viduam, vel repudiatam, vel meretricem in conjugio acceperint, separari eos a proprio episcopo oportebit." — Mansi, *Sacrorum Conciliorum Nova et Amplissima Collectio* (53 vols. in 60, Paris-Leipzig-Arnhem, 1901-1927), X, 630 (hereafter cited Mansi).

11. Stephanus IV ad Carolum et Carolomannum: "Vos adjuramus ... ut nullo modo quisquam de vestra fraternitate praesumat filiam iam dicti Desiderii Lonovardorum regis in conjugium accipere; nec iterum vestra nobilissima germana, Deo amabilis Gisila, tribuatur filio saepefati Desiderii.... Et si quis ... contra hujusmodi nostrae adjurationis atque exhortationis seriem agere praesumpserit, sciat se auctoritate domini mei beati Petri apostolorum principis anathematis vinculo esse innodatum." — Mansi, XII, 697; Migne, *Patrologiae Cursus Completus, Series Latina* (221 vols., Parisiis, 1844-1864), LXXXIX, 1253; XCVIII, 255 (hereafter cited *MPL*); Jaffé, *Regesta Pontificum Romanorum ab condita Ecclesia ad annum post Christum natum MCXCVIII* (2. ed., correctam et auctam auspiciis Gulielmi Wattenbach, curaverunt S. Loewenfeld, F. Kaltenbrunner, P. Ewald, 2 toms. in 1 vol., Lipsiae: Veit, et Comp., 1885-1888), n. 2381 (hereafter cited Jaffé).

to take a vow of chastity or to marry one of her own people within a period of twenty days.[12]

Still later, in the Council of Rheims (1049), Leo IX (1049-1054) forbade Baldwin V (1012-1067), the Count of Flanders, to allow his daughter Mathilda to marry William, the Duke of Normandy.[13]

However, the first express mention of the Church's ban in the nature of a matrimonial impediment is to be found in the writings of Rolandus Bandinelli (later Alexander III).[14] Therefore, at least

---

12. "... Quapropter, quia te super his iam constat fuisse apostolicis conventam epistolis et non solum alienigenis nostratum copulas non permittimus, quin potius, si que contractae sunt, a domino serenissimo imperatore, karissimo filio nostro, continuo dissociandas esse jure sancimus, auctoritate Dei omnipotentis sanctorumque apostolorum principum et nostra praecipimus, ut accepto viginti dierum spacio aut ex nostralibus cum consensu Orbinantium atque Callensium virum legitima federatione suscipias, aut si fidem defuncto viro tuo servasse appetis, sub sacro velamine castimoniam carnis promittas aut certe cum his, quibus te commisimus, in nostram praesentiam venias, sciens, nisi intra prelatum spacium aut virum aut sacrum velamen aut ad nos veniendi iter susciperis, te cum omnibus fautoribus tuis, usque quo venias, omni communione suspensam." — *Monumenta Germaniae Historica* (*MGH*), *Epistolae,* Tomus VII, Pars Prior, *Johannis VIII Papae Registrum* (ed. Ericus Caspar, Berolini: apud Weidmannos, 1912), p. 278, n. 10; Jaffé, n. 2965.

13. "Interdixit et Balduino comiti Flanderensi, ne filiam suam Wilielmo Nortmanno nuptui daret; et illi ne eam acciperet." — Mansi, XIX, 742. Note: Mathilda's paternal grandfather (Baldwin IV [980-1035]) had married William's aunt (the sister of Robert I [† 1035]), and thus William and Mathilda were related in the second degree of the collateral line touching the third. William's father and Mathilda's father were first cousins. This could have been the reason for the ban against the proposed marriage. Actually, this marriage did follow in 1053.

14. "Non oportet (cap. 10) et post: Quod si factum fuerit etc. Hoc ad terrorem dictum neminem latere debet, vel loquitur de his qui contra prohibitionem ecclesiae specialem ex contemptu id agere praedictis temporibus non recusant." — *Die Summa Magistri Rolandi,* nachmals Papst Alexander III, nebst einem Anhange, Incerti Auctoris Quaestiones (Innsbruck, 1874, herausgegeben von Dr. Friederich Thaner), Causa XXXIII, Qu. IV, p. 196.

from the time of Alexander III (1159-1181), this ecclesiastical ban came to be looked upon as a special prohibitive impediment, and as such it received particular attention.[15]

15. Cc. 1, 2, 3, X, *de iis qui contrahunt matrimonium contra interdictum ecclesiae,* IV, 16; Bernardus Papiensis, *Summa Decretalium,* tit. *de matrimonio contra interdictum ecclesiae contracto* (IV, 17), p. 2.

CHAPTER II

HISTORICAL DEVELOPMENT PRIOR TO THE COUNCIL OF TRENT

ARTICLE I. THE AUTHOR OF THE BAN

It is not called for here to vindicate the Church in its restriction of certain individuals from the exercise of the natural right to enter a matrimonial contract. That belongs to another field. The interest of this work is centered simply on the various Church authorities who actually exercised such prohibitive power.

SECTION 1. *The Supreme Pontiff*

As Vicar of Christ and Successor of St. Peter, the Bishop of Rome necessarily enjoys supreme jurisdiction over the Universal Church in matters of faith and morals as well as in things that pertain to the discipline and government of the Church. Consequently, whenever the common good of the Church demands it, the Pope can establish impediments which may be perpetual, either as diriment, or as simply prohibitive. And if he can impose a perpetual matrimonial ban on a certain class of the faithful, then, a fortiori, the supreme lawgiver can issue a temporary prohibition which forbids to some designated individual the celebration of a specific marriage.

Thus Hostiensis († 1271) indicated that sometimes a prohibition of this sort was made in the form of a canon, that is, when the Pope issued a constitution prohibiting the celebration of marriage.[1] At times this prohibition induced only a temporary impediment: in such a case it impeded the matrimonial contract but did not destroy it. At other times, according to Hostiensis, such a papal prohibition induced a perpetual impediment, which not only impeded the matrimonial contract, but broke it completely.[2] As an example of this latter type

1. Hostiensis, *Summa Aurea,* tit. *de matrimonio contra interdictum ecclesiae contracto,* p. 317, n. 2.

2. In the terminology of the glossators a diriment impediment was known as perpetual, while an impedient impediment was called temporary. — *Glossa Ordinaria,* ad c. 4, X, *de sponsa duorum,* IV, 4, s. v. *poteris irritare.*

of prohibition he cited Chapter 21 of Question III under Cause XXXV in the *Decree* of Gratian.[3] Thus it appears that Hostiensis employed the term "prohibition" in both the strict and the wide sense.

However, there was disagreement relative to the point of validity or of invalidity in a marriage contracted in contravention of the Roman Pontiff's prohibition in the strict sense. It is true that at first sight certain decrees seemed to attribute a nullifying effect to a violation of the ordinary papal precept. The first of these is an excerpt from an alleged letter of Pope Celestine I (422-432) to the Church of Florence, and is contained in the *Decree* of Gratian. In part it states: "Quod contra interdictum et ordinem ecclesiae factum est, ratum non haberi tam divinae, quam humanae legis proclamat auctoritas."[4] The second of these texts is contained in the decretal law of Gregory IX, in a letter of Innocent III to Conrad and Peter Malebranche:

> ... quod si contra interdictum nostrum in praeiudicium ipsius (puellae) aliquid fuerit attentatum, id irritum esse decernimus, et viribus omnino carere.[5]

Apparently this latter text proclaims the invalidity of a forbidden marriage — but such is not the case. The glossator, in commenting on this *capitulum,* explained that the word *"irritum"* referred to the *"iudicium, quod movetur in praeiudicium ipsius."*[6] He further stated:

> Secus esset si clausula illa non opponatur: licet mandet Papa aliquid fieri. Sed quid si contraherent matrimonium contra interdictum Papae, numquid irritabitur matrimonium? Dico quod non:

---

3. "Contradicimus, ut in quarta, vel in quinta, sextaque generatione nullus amplius coniugio copuletur. Ubi autem post interdictum factum fuerit inventum, separetur." — C. 21, C. XXXV, q. 3; Mansi, XIV, 75, c. 54.

4. C. 2, C. XXXV, q. 6; Jaffé, n. 384.

5. C. 13, X, *de desponsatione impuberum,* IV, 2; Comp. III, c. 1, h. t., IV, 2 — Potthast, *Regesta Pontificum Romanorum inde ab anno post Christum natum MCXCVIII ad annum MCCCIV,* 2 vols. (Berolini, 1874-1875), n. 535 (hereafter cited Potthast).

6. *Glossa Ordinaria,* ad c. 13, X, *de desponsatione impuberum,* IV, 2, s. v. *irritum.*

sed separabuntur ad tempus quousque cognoscatur de impedimento. Nam fortius est matrimonium quam interdictum Papae.[7]

The original text of Innocent III reads as follows:

> ... Quocira nec accusatio locum habebat, cum non esset quod posset legitime accusari: denunciari tamen poterat consanguinitas, ut interdiceretur matrimonium contrahendum. Ad denunciationem ergo legitime comprobandum festum Omnium Sanctorum proximo venturum pro termino assignamus; salvis exceptionibus non solum propositis sed etiam proponendis. Ne vero quidquam interim in puellam carnaliter attentetur, auctoritate apostolica firmiter interdicimus ut in ipso negotio de novo non procedatur ulterius donec vel a denunciatione cessetur vel, denunciatione probata, ordine iudiciario procedatur. Quod si contra interdictum nostrum in praejudicium ipsius quidquam fuerit attentatum, illud irritum esse decernimus et viribus omnino carere.[8]

Thus, in reality, this decretal of Innocent III did not in any way refer to the nullity of the subsequent marriage contract, but rather to the judicial procedure then in progress, which tended to be prejudicial to the best interests of one of the parties concerned.

Furthermore, as if in refutation of the apparently invalidating effect of a papal precept, the first authentic declaration of law dealing explicitly with this matrimonial impediment decreed such a marriage to be validly contracted:

> ... Licet enim contra interdictum ecclesiae ad secunda vota transire non debuerit, non est tamen conveniens, ut ob id solum sacramentum coniugii dissolvatur. Alia tamen poenitentia eis debebit imponi, quia contra prohibitionem ecclesiae hoc fecerunt.[9]

Commenting on this, the glossator stated: "Sic patet quod interdictum ecclesiae non dissolvit matrimonium, quia non est perpetuum

---

7. *Loc. cit.*

8. *MPL,* CCXIV, *Innocentii III Romani Pontificis Opera Omnia,* Tomus Primus, p. 290, n. CCCXXV; Potthast, n. 535.

9. Alexander III to the Bishops of Winchester, Bath, and Hereford — C. 2, X, *de matrimonio contracto contra interdictum ecclesiae,* IV, 16; Comp. I, c. 3, h. t., IV, 17; Jaffé, n. 14311.

impedimentum, sed poenitentia debet ei imponi quia mandatum ecclesiae contempsit."[10] Abbas Panormitanus (Nicolaus de Tudeschis) (1386-1453) maintained the same doctrine in slightly different language: "Nota quod solum interdictum ecclesiae, factum ex impedimento non perpetuo, non dirimit matrimonium post contractum."[11]

As a result of these apparently conflicting texts and teachings, there was doubt in some quarters as to whether the Supreme Pontiff could impose a precept which would render a marriage invalid. Another of the reasons for doubting the ability of the Holy Father to impose such a precept was the argument that the Church could not change the matter and form of the sacraments. Since matrimony was a sacrament, the Church was not able to vary its matter and form by incapacitating those who by the law of nature were capable of entering marriage.[12]

The solutions which the writers proposed to this problem were both numerous and varied. However, the correct answer was that the ordinary precept imposed by the Supreme Pontiff was merely prohibitive, but that it was within his power to attach to it an invalidating clause. Sylvester Prierias quoted Petrus de Palude to this effect:

> Quod si inhibitio facta fuit ab inferiore a Papa, ut ab episcopo, vel parochiali: quamvis sit peccatum, tamen si non est aliud impedimentum, intellige perpetuum, tenet; et idem si a Papa facta est simpliciter; secus si prohibuerit decernendo irritum et inane si secus factum fuerit, quia est nullum, cum per hoc reddat eos inhabiles, sicut et prohibendo matrimonium per cognationem legalem, spiritualem, vel carnalem in gradu non prohibito lege divina, huiusmodi reddit inhabiles.[13]

---

10. *Glossa Ordinaria,* ad c. 2, X, *de matrimonio contracto contra interdictum ecclesiae,* IV, 16, s. v. *ob id.*

11. Abbatis Panormitani, *Omnia Quae Extant Commentaria* (8 vols., Venetiis, 1588), tit. *de matrimonio contra interdictum ecclesiae contracto,* VII, 63, c. II, n. 3 (hereafter cited *Commentaria*).

12. As quoted by Sanchez, *De Sancti Matrimonii Sacramento Disputationum Tomi Tres* (Antverpiae, 1626), Lib. VII, Disp. I, n. 1 (hereafter cited *De Matrimonio*).

13. *Summa Sylvestrina,* Pars Secunda, *Matrimonium,* VI, p. 147, n. 1.

However, since the maintenance of the proper discipline through the right exercise of power necessitated the application of authority in conformity with the prescriptions of the common law, there existed the presumption that the legislator's acts were in harmony with the common law. And since ordinarily a marriage when contracted in disregard of the papal prohibition was regarded valid, a pontifical precept with an invalidating clause constituted an extraordinary procedure in this matter. Hence, unless the contrary was expressly stated, the ordinary precept imposed by the Pope was merely prohibitive, and not diriment, in character. Nevertheless, in virtue of his apostolic authority, the supreme legislator was competent to attach an invalidating clause to his precept.[14] In this way the alleged letter of Pope Celestine I, which was cited previously, could be satisfactorily explained as containing a papal prohibition to which a nullifying clause had been attached.[15]

From this it followed as a logical corrollary that the Supreme Pontiff had the power to dispense any and all from this prohibition, regardless of the authority by which it had been imposed.[16]

SECTION 2. *The Local Bishop*

In the early days of the Church, local bishops were actually granted the faculty by law of establishing diriment impediments.[17] Subsequently this faculty was revoked, and a local bishop was unable to establish a diriment impediment, even in his own diocese.[18]

---

14. Hostiensis, *Summa Aurea,* tit. *de matrimonio contra interdictum ecclesiae contracto,* p. 317, n. 2.

15. Bernardus Papiensis, *Summa Decretalium,* tit. *de matrimonio contra interdictum ecclesiae contracto* (IV, 17), p. 181, n. 2.

16. "In illis vero impedimentis quae sunt ex statuto ecclesiae cuiusmodi est impedimentum interdicti ecclesiae . . . Papa dispensare potest." —*Summa Sylvestrina,* Pars Secunda, *Matrimonium,* VI, p. 146, n. 5.

17. Pontius, *De Sacramento Matrimonii Tractatus* (Venetiis, 1756), Lib. VI, Cap. VII, p. 227, n. 2.

18. Prosperus Fagnanus, *Commentaria in Quinque Libros Decretalium* (4 vols., Venetiis, 1696), Lib. IV, tit. *de matrimonio contracto contra interdictum ecclesiae,* p. 76, n. 10 (hereafter cited *Commentaria*).

However, as the proper pastor and ordinary judge in his diocese, the bishop was competent to issue a temporary prohibition forbidding a certain marriage ceremony.[19] And to this precept he was empowered to add the threat of an excommunication.[20] Thus Alexander III wrote that the bishop was competent to forbid litigant consorts to contract a second marriage the while the validity of their first marriage was being contested.[21] In doing this the bishop was but fulfilling a provision enjoined by an earlier decretal of the same pontiff. This decree ordered that when the validity of a former marriage was being investigated, the consorts were to be commanded not to contract a new marriage, even though they themselves were well aware of the invalidity of their marriage.[22]

The common law of the Church recognized the bishop as the sole competent authority to take cognizance of matrimonial causes, and questions regarding the sacrament of matrimony were brought to him

---

19. Bernardus Papiensis, *Summa Decretalium,* tit. *de matrimonio contra interdictum ecclesiae contracto* (IV, 17), p. 181.

20. "Sed cum archiepiscopus velit cognoscere de primo matrimonio, mulier ad sedem apostolica appellavit: archiepiscopus ejus appellationi deferens, praecepit eidem mulieri sub poena excommunicationis, ne alicui nuberet, donec causa finem debitum sortiretur." — *Glossa Ordinaria,* ad c. 2, X, *de matrimonio contracto contra interdictum ecclesiae,* IV, 16, s. v. *casus.*

21. Alexander III to the Bishop of Padua: "Mandamus, quatenus si est ita, praefatam mulierem (ne mandatum tuum contemptibile videatur) ad domum matris redire compellas, et imposita sibi de tanto excessu poenitentia condigna, postquam in domo materna per mensem steterit, ad tertium reverti permittas." — C. 1, X, *de matrimonio contracto contra interdictum ecclesiae,* IV, 16; Comp. I, c. 2, h. t., IV, 17; Jaffé, n. 14055.

22. Alexander III to the Archbishop of Genoa: "De his vero, qui coram te super desponsatione, factum per consensum mutuum de praesenti, controversiam movent, et appellatione pendente, quam ante sententiam vel cognitionem causae ad sedem apostolicam interponunt, accipiunt alias in uxores, hoc arbitramur agendum, ut, si amodo in tali casu duxerint appellandum, eis in ecclesia publice interdicas arctius ne ante decisionem causae aliud contrahant matrimonium. Et si contra interdictum ecclesiae ita publice factum venire praesumpserint, matrimonium tam praesumptuose contractum poteris irritare." — C. 4, X, *de sponsa duorum,* IV, 4; Comp. I, c. 9, h. t., IV, 4; Jaffé, n. 13969.

for proper settlement.[23] Thus Petrus de Palude referred to the bishop as the one who had competence to prohibit a marriage, since it was he who possessed power not only of a judicial but also of an administrative character.[24]

Although the bishop possessed the necessary faculty of issuing a temporary mandate restraining two people from intermarrying, he was without competency to add an invalidating clause to his order. This he could have done only if he had been competent to establish diriment impediments. That he was not competent to do so was demonstrated by the fact that marriages which had been contracted in spite of an episcopal interdict were decreed to be valid.[25] In conformity with such decisions, Panormitanus firmly taught that the mere interdict of the Church, when imposed as an impediment which was not perpetual, did not invalidate a marriage contracted afterwards.[26]

It seems, then, that at the time of Alexander III no ecclesiastical dignitary subordinate to the Supreme Pontiff was qualified to institute diriment impediments. Yet there was no decree in existence that reserved this right exclusively to the Vicar of Christ. Two possible explanations for the actual reservation of this power to the Supreme Pontiff suggest themselves. Either the establishment of diriment im-

---

23. "Aliquando iudex qui de hac causa cognoscere potest, cum enim matrimonium magnum sacramentum sit in ecclesia Dei, non potest de ipso cognoscere de iure communi, nisi sit episcopus." — Hostiensis, *Summa Aurea,* tit. *de matrimonio contra interdictum ecclesiae contracto,* p. 317, n. 2.

24. "Minister ad interdicendum matrimonium est . . . episcopus . . . qui habet judicare ratione jurisdictionis, et dispensare ratione ordinis cum cura." — *Summa Sylvestrina,* Pars Secunda, *Matrimonium,* VI, p. 147, n. 1.

25. "Licet enim contra interdictum ecclesiae ad secunda vota transire non debuerit, non est tamen conveniens ut ob id solum sacramentum coniugii dissolvatur. Alia tamen poenitentia eis debebit imponi, quia contra prohibitionem ecclesiae hoc fecerunt." — *Corpus Iuris Canonici* (ed. Lipsiensis 2, post Aemilii Ludovici Richteri curas . . . instruxit Aemilius Friedberg, 2 vols., Lipsiae: Tauchnitz, 1879-1881; ed. anastatice repetita, 1928), c. 2, X, *de matrimonio contracto contra interdictum ecclesiae,* IV, 16.

26. "Nota quod solum interdictum ecclesiae, factum ex impedimento non perpetuo, non dirimit matrimonium post contractum." — Abbatis Panormitani, *Commentaria,* tit. *de matrimonio contra interdictum ecclesiae contracto,* VII, 63, c. II.

pediments was considered a *causa maior,* and therefore reserved to the Successor of St. Peter,[27] or the reservation resulted from general custom — that custom which shrinks from an ever-changing discipline.

It was within the competency of the bishop to grant a dispensation from a prohibition forbidding a certain marriage ceremony, provided it had been imposed either by himself or by some authority subordinate to himself; not, however, if it had been imposed by a superior authority.[28]

SECTION 3. *The Ecclesiastical Judge*

Since the validity of marriages was often impugned by interested as well as disinterested persons, the alleged reasons of the plaintiff and defendant had to be properly appraised and discreetly judged. This was the function of an ecclesiastical judge. It is evident, therefore, that the judge had to possess the necessary jurisdiction and sufficient knowledge of the law.[29]

Inasmuch as matrimony is "a great sacrament," and the bishop is charged with the custody of the sacraments, he becomes the ordinary judge in his diocese concerning matters pertaining to matrimony.[30] Quite naturally, then, questions about the sacrament of matrimony were referred to the bishop or to his delegate, who was known also as the *missus*[31] or *missus Dominicus.*[32] (In explanation it may be said that *missus* was the term for a Frankish royal officer. However, the glossators used the term to refer to the bishop's *officialis.*[33])

---

27. Vlaming, *Praelectiones Iuris Canonici ad Normam Codicis Iuris Canonici* (3. ed., 2 vols., Bussum in Hollandia: Sumptibus Societatis Editricis Anonymae olim Paulus Brand, 1919-1921), I, p. 159, n. 186, note 2.

28. *Summa Sylvestrina,* Pars Secunda, *Matrimonium,* VI, p. 146, n. 6.

29. *Glossa Ordinaria,* ad c. 1, X, *de consanguinitate et affinitate,* IV, 14, s. v. *casus.*

30. C. 1, D. XXV.

31. C. 1, X, *de frigidis et maleficiatis, et impotentia coeundi,* IV, 15; Comp. I, c. 1, h. t., IV, 16.

32. C. 2, X, *de regularibus et transeuntibus ad religionem,* III, 31; Comp. I, c. 2, h. t., III, 27.

33. Hostiensis, *Summa Aurea,* tit. *de matrimonio contra interdictum ecclesiae contracto,* p. 317, n. 2.

Not only was the ecclesiastical judge competent to issue an injunction to prevent the contracting of a second marriage when the validity of the first was being contested, but he was under a legal obligation to command that such a step be put into effect.[34] But since he was merely a subordinate of the principal legislator, who alone was capable of invalidating a marriage contracted in disregard of his injunction, the judge was incompetent to attach a nullifying clause to his prohibition.[35]

A strict interpretation of Alexander III's decretal on the competence of ecclesiastical judges in matrimonial causes[36] led Goffredus de Trano († 1245) and others to maintain that only an ecclesiastical judge was authorized to enjoin a prohibition against the contracting of a marriage.[37]

An obvious objection to this interpretation was the fact that according to the decretal law even a parish priest had an obligation to forbid a specific marriage from being contracted whenever the circumstances of the case warranted such a prohibition.[38]

But before entering into the question of the competence of the parish priest in this matter, we may well consider the decretal law as to the competence enjoyed by Church dignitaries who acted as

34. C. 4, X, *de sponsa duorum,*. IV, 4; Comp. I, c. 9, h. t., IV, 4; Jaffé, n. 13969; Abbatis Panormitani, *Commentaria,* tit. *de matrimonio contra interdictum ecclesiae contracto,* VII, p. 63, c. III, n. 2.

35. Abbatis Panormitani, *Commentaria,* tit. *de matrimonio contra interdictum ecclesiae contracto,* VII, p. 62, c. I, n. 1; *Glossa Ordinaria,* ad c. 4, X, *de sponsa duorum,* IV, 4, s. v. *poteris irritare.*

36. C. 1, X, *de consanguinitate et affinitate,* IV, 14; Comp. I, c. 2, h. t., IV, 14; Jaffé, n. 13838.

37. Goffredus de Trano, *Summa,* tit. *de matrimonio contracto contra interdictum ecclesiae,* n. 1 — as quoted by Sanchez, *De Matrimonio,* Lib. VII, Disp. VI, n. 6; Hostiensis, *Summa Aurea,* tit. *de matrimonio contra interdictum ecclesiae contracto,* p. 317, n. 2; *Summa Sylvestrina,* Pars Secunda,. *Matrimonium,* VI, p. 147, n. 1.

38. "Si vero parochialis sacerdos tales conjunctiones prohibere contempserit aut interesse praesumpserit, per triennium ab officio suspendatur." — *Glossa Ordinaria,* ad c. 3, X, *de clandestina desponsatione,* IV, 3, s. v. *casus.* Cf. *Summa Sylvestrina,* Pars Secunda, *Matrimonium,* VI, p. 147, n. 1.

judges, ordinary or delegate. Thus we find that the cathedral chapter also was competent to give a precept in this matter, but only when the see was vacant.[39] So, too, were the archdeacon and the archpriest, but only upon delegation or through custom.[40] In addition, any minister of the Church was competent to give a precept prohibiting a marriage if he had a special mandate of the bishop to that effect, or if he already possessed this power through long-standing custom.[41]

However, the above-mentioned dignitaries were incompetent to give a precept invalidating a marriage if it was contracted in disregard of their prohibition.

SECTION 4. *The Parish Priest*

Regarding the authority capable of issuing a limited matrimonial prohibition, another and somewhat disputed point concerned the competence of the parish priest in the matter. Among the Gregorian Decretals was a decree issued by Alexander III to the abbot of Monte Cassino, which gave the norm to be observed in matrimonial causes — namely, matrimonial causes were not to be handled by anyone except discreet judges who enjoyed the necessary judicial power.[42]

As has already been observed, Goffredus de Trano, relying on a strict interpretation of this text, concluded that an ecclesiastical judge was the sole competent authority constituted by law to take cognizance

39. Hostiensis, *Summa Aurea,* tit. *de matrimonio contra interdictum ecclesiae contracto,* p. 317, n. 2.

40. "Forte ad hoc delegato, vel de loci consuetudine, quae tribuit jurisdictionem." — *Glossa Ordinaria,* ad c. 1, X, *de consanguinitate et affinitate,* IV, 14, s.v. *coram archipresbytero;* Comp. I, c. 2, h.t., IV, 14; Jaffé, n. 13838. Cf. Bernardus Papiensis, *Summa Decretalium,* tit. *de matrimonio contra interdictum ecclesiae contracto* (IV, 17), p. 181, n. 2; Hostiensis, *In Quinque Libros Decretalium Commentaria* (5 vols. in 3, Venetiis, 1581), tit. *de restitutione spoliatorum,* II, 13, c. 13, n. 1, s.v. *in tua praesentia* (hereafter cited *Commentaria*).

41. Hostiensis, *Summa Aurea,* tit. *de matrimonio contra interdictum ecclesiae contracto,* p. 317, n. 2.

42. ". . . non sunt causae matrimonii tractandae per quoslibet, sed per iudices discretos, qui potestatem habeant iudicandi, et statuta canonum non ignorant." — C. 1, X, *de consanguinitate et affinitate,* IV, 14; Comp. I, c. 2, h.t., IV, 14; Jaffé, n. 13838.

of matrimonial causes,[43] and that he alone could impose the prohibition that forbade the celebration of a specific marriage.

But such a conclusion was not justified. Goffredus' contention that a prohibition could not be made without due cognizance of the cause, and that such did not fall within the sphere of the parish priest's power, was valid only in regard to a prohibition issued in causes requiring a judicial process for their proper adjudication. Granted that the ecclesiastical judge alone was capable of *adjudicating* matrimonial causes; still, the power *to forbid* a specific marriage was actually exercised by the parish priest. In fact, he was obliged to do so ex officio.[44]

The problem, then, is to reconcile these two facts. The difference in the two procedures which served to bring about the same desired end is to be found in the fact that the judge issued his prohibition in a judicial manner, whereas the parish priest forbade the marriage in an extrajudicial manner, and without any decision as to the existence or nonexistence of an alleged impediment. Hence, it was irrelevant to object that the imposition of the precept always implied an act of judicial jurisdiction, which could be exercised solely by the bishop, and not by the parish priest. That the contrary did obtain is deducible from the existing legislation current in the decretal period.

Intent on outlawing the rampant evil of clandestine marriages, the IV General Council of the Lateran (1215), held under Innocent III, enacted the celebrated decree *Cum inhibitio.* In part it reads as follows:

> Et ipsi presbyteri nihilominus investigent, utrum aliquod impedimentum obsistat. Cum autem apparuerit probabilis coniectura contra copulam contrahendam, contractus expresse interdicatur, donec, quid fieri debeat super eo, manifestis constiterit documentis.[45]

---

43. Goffredus de Trano, *Summa,* tit. *de matrimonio contracto contra interdictum ecclesiae,* n. 1 — as cited by Sanchez, *De Matrimonio,* Lib. VII, Disp. VI, n. 6.

44. C. 3, X, *de clandestina desponsatione,* IV, 3; Conc. Lateranen. IV (1215), can. 51; Comp. IV, c. 1, h. t., IV, 2.

45. Conc. Lateranen. IV (1215), can. 51 — Mansi, XX, 1038.

This conciliar legislation was later incorporated into the decretal law of Gregory IX.[46]

In its decree the Council spoke of "*presbyteri.*" The lack of any gloss on this word seems to indicate a unanimity among the glossators as to the meaning of "*presbyteri.*" The term referred to regular as well as to secular priests.[47] Desirous of manifesting its intention of including the regular clergy under the term "*presbyteri,*" the same Council explicitly mentioned the regulars when it established sanctions against the violation of its fifty-first canon. The obligation to forbid certain marriages was clearly indicated in the conclusion of the same decree:

> Sane si parochialis sacerdos tales coniunctiones prohibere contempserit, aut quilibet etiam regularis qui eis praesumpserit interesse, per triennium ab officio suspendatur, gravius puniendus, si culpae qualitas postulaverit.[48]

Of particular interest is this specific designation of the regular clergy. The latter were expressly singled out by the Council because they were wont to witness such forbidden marriages. They claimed their assistance at such marriages was based on their privilege of exemption. But the Council rectified that mistaken notion.[49]

The Fathers of the Council spoke of the parish priest as the one to be punished for his failure to forbid the celebration of a particular marriage. Now if the priest was to be punished for his negligence, that negligence had to be culpable and imputable; and for it to be imputable, the person blamed had to have it within his power to perform an act which could have prevented the action for which he was

46. C. 3, X, *de clandestina desponsatione,* IV, 3; Conc. Lateranen. IV (1215), can. 51; Comp. IV, c. 1, h. t., IV, 2.

47. Hostiensis, *Commentaria,* tit. *de clandestina desponsatione* (IV, 3), c. 3, n. 4.

48. C. 3, X, *de clandestina desponsatione,* IV, 3; Conc. Lateranen. IV (1215), can. 51; Comp. IV, c. 1, h. t., IV, 2. Cf. Hostiensis, *Commentaria,* tit. *de clandestina desponsatione* (IV, 3), c. 3, n. 4, s. v. *prohibere.*

49. "Etiam si exemptus sit. Nam et hi praetextu exemptionis talia consueverunt impune committere. Hodie tamen in talibus punientur." — Hostiensis, *Commentaria,* tit. *de clandestina desponsatione* (IV, 3), c. 3, n. 4, s. v. *regularis.*

being blamed and punished. It thus becomes evident that according to the then existing law the parish priest was competent to impose this prohibitive matrimonial impediment.

From this conciliar legislation it must be concluded that not only could the parish priest temporarily prohibit a marriage from taking place, but that in certain circumstances he actually had an obligation to do so.[50] In the meantime, the matter was to be duly investigated and properly adjudicated by the ordinary judge in the exercise of his authority relative to matrimony.

Although the parish priest and the regular clergy were mentioned by the Council, a more specific determination of this terminology seems not to have been made. It is certain that at least there was reference to the pastors.[51] Church history reveals that at this time there was a complete dismemberment and dissolution of the so-called "grand parishes." The greater portion of the filial churches had already attained the status of parochial churches. This increase in parishes necessitated a greater number of priests to take charge of the newly formed parishes, and the Church had to assign one priest to each parish. The only exception to this practice was to be found in the larger city parishes. Consequently, if the decree of the IV Lateran Council on clandestine and forbidden marriages was to have any effect, it was necessary that the pastor have the power to forbid the celebration of a marriage whenever the occasion demanded.

Then, too, in medieval language the term *sacerdos* or *presbyter parochialis* was distinctive of the pastor.[52] Thus the Council must have intended him when it made reference in its decree *Cum inhibitio* to the *sacerdos* and *presbyter parochialis*. Accordingly, there can be no doubt that pastors could temporarily forbid the celebration of a marriage.

---

50. C. 3, X, *de clandestina desponsatione,* IV, 3; Conc. Lateranen. IV (1215), can. 51; Comp. IV, c. 1, h. t., IV, 2.

51. Gasparri, *Tractatus Canonicus de Matrimonio* (2 vols., Parisiis, 1891), n. 141.

52. Bastnagel, Clement, *The Appointment of Parochial Adjutants and Assistants,* The Catholic University of America Canon Law Studies, n. 58 (Washington, D. C.: The Catholic University of America, 1930), p. 28.

In regard to the competence of the assistant clergy to give a precept temporarily forbidding a particular couple to contract marriage, the situation is not quite so clear. The IV Lateran Council did not refer to them. In view of the situation as it existed in regard to the pastor, it seems logical to conclude that the assistant clergy did not enjoy the faculty of imposing this matrimonial impediment. At least, Bernard of Pavia came to this conclusion.[53]

But even though in his own right the assistant priest was absolutely incompetent in this matter, he could, nevertheless, be delegated by the pastor.[54] Therefore, it seems that in this matter the assistant clergy had no competency except upon an act of proper delegation.

ARTICLE II. THE CANONICAL STATUS OF MARRIAGES CONTRACTED IN CONTRAVENTION OF THIS BAN

Although much was said by many in regard to the canonical status of such marriages — some of it seemingly contradictory — it may be safely said that, in general, canonically forbidden marriages were decreed to be valid but illicit.[55]

However, the existence of certain decretals which seemingly attributed an invalidating effect to such a legitimate precept gave rise to some doubts. One of these texts, written by Alexander III, reads as follows: "Si contra interdictum ecclesiae publice factum venire praesumpserint, matrimonium tam praesumtuose contractum poteris irritare."[56] The difficulty of interpretation derives from the use of the words "*poteris irritare.*" The glossator pointed out that these words

---

53. "Non autem credo quemlibet cappellanum tale posse facere interdictum." — Bernardus Papiensis, *Summa,* tit. *de matrimonio contra interdictum ecclesiae contracto* (IV, 17), p. 181, n. 2.

54. ". . . nisi hoc faceret auctoritate illius ad quem spectat." — *Loc. cit.*

55. "Ita tenendum est sine aliqua dubitatione quod illi, quorum matrimonium interdictur, non debent contrahere; sed si contrahunt, nisi aliud impedimentum impediat, possunt simul permanere, et non sunt separandi, nisi ad tempus, ut agant poenitentiam." — Raymundus de Pennafort, *Summa* (Veronae, 1744), tit. XVIII, *De matrimonio contra interdictum ecclesiae celebrato,* p. 519 (hereafter cited as S. Raymundi *Summa*).

56. C. 4, X, *de sponsa duorum,* IV, 4; Comp. I, c. 9, h. t., IV, 4; Jaffé, n. 13969.

were to be interpreted differently according to different circumstances.[57]

In other words, the cause of the prohibition determined the status of the marriage. If the prohibition had been imposed because of some perpetual cause, the marriage was both illicit and invalid.[58] Therefore, the would-be consorts were to be separated, and if the existence of an alleged invalidating cause was verified, a sentence of nullity was to be pronounced.[59] On the other hand, if some temporary cause had been the motive for the prohibition, then the marriage was valid but illicit.[60]

Thus it is evident that ordinarily the phrase "*poteris irritare*" was not to be interpreted in its strict acceptation. In other words, the prohibition usually did not exceed the limits of a prohibitive impediment. And this view was to be maintained in spite of the fact that there were cases in which marriages were declared invalid when this canonical impediment was apparently involved. For in such cases a thorough examination of the facts revealed that the marriages were declared invalid not because of the ecclesiastical prohibition but because of the presence of some diriment impediment.

Obviously, then, the word "*irritare*" was to be interpreted as not necessarily calling for anything more than the separation of the consorts, and as relating primarily, not to the prohibited marriage itself, but to the nature of the cause underlying the banning of the marriage.[61]

---

57. *Glossa Ordinaria,* ad c. 4, X, *de sponsa duorum,* IV, 4, s. v. *poteris irritare.*

58. "Si causa est perpetua, separantur a cohabitatione quousque cognoscatur de impedimento, quo probato separantur ex toto, lata sententia divortii inter eos." — *Loc. cit.*

59. "Inter eos sententiam divortii non differas promulgare." — C. 4, X, *de desponsatione impuberum,* IV, 2; Comp. I, c. 5, h. t., IV, 2; Jaffé, n. 13947.

60. "Si vero causa prohibitionis fuerit temporalis . . . tunc non deberent separari. . . . Interdictum enim ecclesiae non est tantae efficaciae ut separetur matrimonium contra illud contractum, nisi subsit causa perpetua." — *Glossa Ordinaria,* ad c. 4, X, *de sponsa duorum,* IV, 4, s. v. *poteris irritare.*

61. "Tamen ne mandatum iudicis contemptibile videatur, si vult, potest eos ad tempus separare. . . . Interdictum enim ecclesiae non est tantae efficaciae ut separetur matrimonium contra illud contractum, nisi subsit causa perpetua." — *Loc. cit.*

Opposed to doubtful texts such as the one written by Alexander III were the decretals which treated explicitly of the matrimonial impediment here under discussion.[62] As far as these decretals are concerned, the proof that marriages contracted in violation of this prohibition were nevertheless deemed valid is overwhelming. The glossators stated it explicitly;[63] and the commentators on the Decretals maintained it again and again.[64]

William Durantis (1237-1296) summed up the whole controversy in these words: "Scias quod interdictum ecclesiae non est tantae efficaciae ut matrimonium contra id contractus, si alias legitimum est, separetur."[65] And St. Raymond de Pennafort (1175-1275) held that without a doubt such marriages were valid, but illicit. Well aware of the interpretations which had been given to the various decrees treating of this matrimonial impediment, he wrote: "Si vero aliqua inveniuntur decreta quae dicunt taliter coniunctos esse separandos, exponenda est littera quod ad tempus sunt separandi."[66]

Thus it is evident that both the decretal law and the decretalists proclaimed the validity of marriages that had been contracted in contravention of the prohibition of the Church. This matrimonial impediment, then, was merely a prohibitive impediment—unless in issuing the prohibition the Supreme Pontiff had expressly attached an invalidating clause to the precept.[67]

---

62. Cc. 1, 2, 3, X, *de matrimonio contracto contra interdictum ecclesiae,* IV, 16.

63. "Sic patet quod interdictum ecclesiae non dissolvit matrimonium quia non est perpetuum impedimentum." —*Glossa Ordinaria,* ad c. 2, X, *de matrimonio contra interdictum ecclesiae contracto,* IV, 16, s. v. *ob id.*

64. Abbatis Panormitani *Commentaria,* tit. *de matrimonio contra interdictum ecclesiae contracto,* VII, 62, c. I, n. 1; Bernardus Papiensis, *Summa Decretalium,* tit. *De sponsalibus et matrimoniis,* p. 131, n. 6; Hostiensis, *Summa Aurea,* tit. *De sponsalibus et matrimoniis,* p. 291, n. 27 b.

65. Gulielmus Durantis, *Speculum Judiciale* (Venetiis, 1577), Lib. IV, Partic. IV, p. 49, § *scias.*

66. S. Raymundi *Summa,* tit. XVIII, *De matrimonio contra interdictum ecclesiae celebrato,* p. 519.

67. *Summa Sylvestrina,* Pars Secunda, *Matrimonium,* VI, p. 147, n. 1.

ARTICLE III. CAUSES FOR THE ISSUANCE OF A VALID BAN

It was only natural that the question should arise as to whether the prohibition was of valid effect if it was imposed without a just cause. Some of the authors held an affirmative view in regard to pontifical prohibitions, although they considered it blameworthy for the Pope if he acted without a just cause.[68]

However, the truth of the matter was that since the postponement of a marriage could occasion serious consequences, the act of imposing a precept in this matter required a just cause. In fact, if the precept was imposed without a just cause, it was null and void.[69]

If a just cause existed, it necessarily was either of a temporary or of a perpetual character. A marriage contracted in violation of a temporary cause was certainly illicit, but nevertheless valid. On the other hand, if a marriage was contracted in violation of a perpetual cause, the marriage was invalid unless a dispensation had been obtained.[70]

To determine what constituted a just cause — one sufficient to warrant the imposing of this interdict — it is necessary to consult the decretal law of Gregory IX. Scattered throughout numerous passages one finds mention of various causes for which a specific marriage could be temporarily forbidden. For instance, the general belief that a perpetual impediment existed was definitely considered a sufficient cause for imposing such a temporary prohibition.[71]

This general belief, or *fama,* as it was called, did not have to be founded on a fact which was itself well-known. Even if the fact giving rise to the general belief was occult or private, it was sufficient to

---

68. Hostiensis, *Commentaria,* tit. *de sponsa duorum* (IV, 4), c. 4, n. 1, s. v. *irritare.*

69. "... aut interdictum fit sine causa, et tunc nullum est interdictum." — Hostiensis, *Summa Aurea,* tit. *de matrimonio contra interdictum ecclesiae contracto,* p. 317, n. 3.

70. "Aut causa est temporalis aut perpetua. Si temporalis ... non est contrahendum matrimonium, contractum tamen tenet.... Si perpetua, aut vera aut falsa. Si vera, incontinenti separantur et negotio examinato perpetuum divortium fertur." — *Loc. cit.*

71. "Nota quod fama impedit matrimonium contrahendum." — *Glossa Ordinaria,* ad c. 2, X, *de consanguinitate et affinitate,* IV, 14, s. v. *fama.*

constitute a cause for prohibiting the marriage.[72] It was possible, therefore, for someone to suffer from general belief of a perpetual impediment though the matter that gave rise to it remained occult.[73] However, the general belief had actually to be in existence. A denunciation alone, without the general belief as a basis for it, was not a sufficient cause for prohibiting a marriage.[74]

A somewhat similar cause, which is more fully treated in a later section,[75] was that of scandal incident to a perpetual impediment. There is no doubt that this type of scandal was also considered a sufficient reason for prohibiting a marriage.[76] In fact, Panormitanus taught that if scandal of this type was greatly to be feared, the judge was not only allowed but was even obligated to forbid the marriage.[77]

Other causes included previous espousals entered into with a third party,[78] the lodging of an appeal concerning the validity of a former

---

72. "Vel etiam si non est notorium, fama tamen loci hoc habet, ille debet ab impetitione ipsius absolvi." — *Glossa Ordinaria,* ad c. 2, X, *de consanguinitate et affinitate,* IV, 14, s. v. *casus;* "Et. sic est fama aliquid quod dicitur occultum sive privatum, et ideo dicitur fama privatum impedimentum: quia per famam solam non constat de impedimento, nisi alia probatio adsit." — *Glossa Ordinaria,* ad c. 27, X, *de sponsalibus et matrimoniis,* IV, 1, s. v. *licet fama privatum.*

73. "Sic ergo nota famam esse de aliquo et tamen id, de quo est, censetur occultum." — Hostiensis, *Commentaria,* tit. *de sponsalibus et matrimoniis* (IV, 1), c. 27, n. 3, s. v. *et de fama.*

74. "Sola denunciatio non impedit matrimonium nisi adsit fama, et ita sola fama impedit matrimonium." — *Glossa Ordinaria,* ad c. 27, X, *de sponsalibus et matrimoniis,* IV, 1, s. v. *de fama.*

75. Cf. pp. 99-101 of this work.

76. "Nota quod propter scandalum impeditur matrimonium." — *Glossa Ordinaria,* ad c. 27, X, *de sponsalibus et matrimoniis,* IV, 1, s. v. *scandalo;* "Iudex . . . debet illos compellere ut a tali contractu desistant, ex quo fama vel scandalum est probatum." — *Ibid.,* s. v. *casus.*

77. ". . . ubi inter aliquas parentelas scandalum vehementer timetur ex contractu matrimonii, potest et debet iudex interdicere matrimonium." — Abbatis Panormitani *Commentaria,* tit. *de sponsalibus et matrimoniis* (VII, 16), c. XXVII, n. 4.

78. "[Archiepiscopus] sub anathematis interminatione prohibuit ne antequam de praescripto negotio [praeviis sponsalibus] plene constaret, vir ad secunda vota transiret." — C. 2, X, *de iis qui contrahunt matrimonium contra interdictum ecclesiae,* IV, 16; Comp. I, c. 3, h. t., IV, 17; Jaffé, n. 14311.

marriage,[79] and a founded suspicion of a latent impediment, whether diriment or prohibitive.[80]

ARTICLE IV. PENALTIES INCURRED FOR THE VIOLATION OF A VALID BAN

SECTION 1. *By the Priest for His Assistance at a Banned Marriage and for His Failure to Forbid Its Celebration*

Making use of its coercive power, the IV General Council of the Lateran enacted grave penalties for the violation of its fifty-first canon. The severest penalties were meted out to a priest who deliberately neglected to prohibit a forbidden marriage or who assisted at one which he knew to be forbidden.[81]

The penalties were incurred if he failed in his duty through contempt, negligence, fear, friendship, entreaties, or bribery — in general, if he did not have a just cause for acting in opposition to the law.[82]

Thus, any priest found guilty in this matter was to be suspended "*ab officio*" for a period of three years. Furthermore, if the nature of the offense merited it, he was to be punished more severely.[83]

---

79. "Hoc arbitramur agendum, ut . . . eis in ecclesia publice interdicas, ne ante decisionem causae, aliud contrahant matrimonium." — C. 4, X, *de sponsa duorum,* IV, 4; Comp. I, c. 9, h. t., IV, 4; Jaffé, n. 13969.

80. "Cum autem apparuerit probabilis coniectura contra copulam contrahendam, contractus interdicatur expresse, donec, quid fieri debeat super eo, manifestis constiterit documentis." — C. 3, X, *de clandestina desponsatione,* IV, 3; Conc. Lateranen. IV (1215), can. 51; Comp. IV, c. 1, h. t., IV, 2. "Nota quod probabilis causa impedit matrimonium contrahendum." — *Glossa Ordinaria,* ad c. 3, X, *de clandestina desponsatione,* IV, 3, s. v. *probabilis coniectura.*

81. C. 3, X, *de clandestina desponsatione,* IV, 3; Conc. Lateranen. IV (1215), can. 51; Comp. IV, c. 1, h. t., IV, 2.

82. Hostiensis, *Summa Aurea,* tit. *de sponsa duorum,* p. 298, n. 9.

83. "Sane, si parochialis sacerdos tales coniunctiones prohibere contempserit, aut quilibet etiam regularis, qui eis praesumpserit interesse, per triennium ab officio suspendatur, gravius puniendus, si culpae qualitas postulaverit." — C. 3, X, *de clandestina desponsatione,* IV, 3; Conc. Lateranen. IV (1215), can. 51; Comp. IV, c. 1, h. t., IV, 2.

The use of the word "*suspendatur*" seems to indicate that the suspension was not incurred *ipso facto,* but that it was, rather, a *ferendae sententiae* penalty. Hence, the sentence had to be pronounced by the ordinary or his delegate. Since the time of the suspension was determined by law, a longer or shorter period could not be imposed. However, once the prescribed penalty had been assigned, the bishop could commute it to a milder sentence whenever the circumstances seemed to warrant this;[84] on the other hand, he could increase the penalty whenever the consideration of justice demanded it in view of the special malice or unusually reprehensible character of the guilt.[85]

From the fact that the "regulars" were mentioned explicitly, it seems evident that even exempt religious could be punished by the ordinary if they violated this canon.[86]

As regards the secular clergy, the pastors incurred this penalty not only if they actually assisted at such a marriage, but even if they knew that such a marriage was to take place and failed to prohibit it. The secular priests other than pastors and the "regulars" did not incur this penalty if they failed to prohibit a marriage — since they were not ex officio bound to do this — but only if they assisted at a marriage which they knew to be forbidden.[87]

In addition, those who maliciously objected to a legitimate marriage in order to have it forbidden, or who maliciously forbade such a legitimate marriage, incurred a special penalty to be determined according to the discretion of the judge. However, any cleric who

---

84. "Numquid mitiorem poenam potest episcopus imponere? Non videtur ab initio, quia ubi certa poena scripta est, non debet iudex mitiorem vel duriorem infligere, alias infamia gravi notabitur . . . sed ea inflicta poterit ad minus dispensare et diminuere secundum quod qualitas personae exigerit." — Hostiensis, *Summa Aurea,* tit. *de clandestina desponsatione,* p. 298, n. 12.

85. ". . . gravius, nam etiam ex eodem facto aliquis plus aliquis minus punitur secundum quod culpa exigit." — *Loc. cit.*

86. *Loc. cit.*

87. *Ibid.,* n. 9.

was found guilty of such a calumnious denunciation was to be suspended *"ab officio et beneficio."*[88]

SECTION 2. *By the Contracting Parties for Their Act Performed in Bad or Doubtful Conscience*

Although the decretals acknowledged as valid any marriage contracted simply in contravention of the prohibition of the Church, nevertheless they decreed that a penance be imposed on the guilty party or parties. Thus the IV Lateran Council decreed that a suitable penance be imposed upon those who presumed to contract marriage against the prohibition of the Church.[89]

It is interesting to note that those who violated this prohibition laid themselves open to the assignment of a penance even though in actuality there was no impediment to the marriage. The punishment was imposed not because the parties sought to contract marriage in the face of an impediment, but because they violated the prohibition of the Church.[90] Since no definite duration for the performance of this penance was indicated in the law, it was left to the discretion of the competent ecclesiastical authority to determine.

While the penance was being performed, the guilty couple were to be temporarily separated.[91] Although in the decretal mention was made of a month's separation of the consorts, that length of time was

---

88. *Glossa Ordinaria,* ad c. 3, X, *de clandestina desponsatione,* IV, 3, s. v. *malitiose;* c. 2, X, *de calumniatoribus,* V, 2; Comp. III, c. 7, *de accusationibus, inquisitionibus et denunciationibus,* V, 1; Potthast, n. 3100.

89. "Condigna poenitentia iniungatur." — C. 3, X, *de clandestina desponsatione,* IV, 3; Conc. Lateranen. IV (1215), can. 51; Comp. IV, c. 1, h. t., IV, 2. Cf. also c. 1, X, *de matrimonio contracto contra interdictum ecclesiae,* IV, 16; Comp. I, c. 2, h. t., IV, 17; Jaffé, n. 14055.

90. "Nota quod puniuntur contrahentes et tamen nullum subest impedimentum, sed illud ideo fit quia contrahunt contra interdictum ecclesiae, unde puniuntur non propter impedimentum, sed quia mandatum ecclesiae contemnunt." — *Glossa Ordinaria,* ad c. 3, X, *de clandestina desponsatione,* IV, 3, s. v. *poenitentia.*

91. "Ad domum matris redire compellas." — C. 1, X, *de matrimonio contracto contra interdictum ecclesiae,* IV, 16; Comp. I, c. 2, h. t., IV, 17; Jaffé, n. 14055.

indicated solely by way of illustration. There was not implied in the decretal any restriction of the power of the competent authority. The separation was to last as long as the pending case remained unresolved.[92]

An additional punishment to be inflicted upon guilty parties was established in a decretal of Pope Urban III, *Cum in Apostolica.* In response to a query of the Bishop of Le Mans, France, regarding the proper measure to be taken concerning those who had contracted a second marriage while the validity of the first marriage was being contested, the Pope decreed that even though subsequent events proved the first marriage to have been invalidly contracted, the accustomed penance was to be imposed, and in addition the consorts were to be deprived of the marital right during the determined penitential period.[93]

Since the Church recognized the injustice of depriving an innocent consort of such a fundamental right if he had not in some way forfeited it, the exercise of the marital right was forbidden both consorts only when both had knowingly proceeded with the marriage against the prohibition of the Church — for in such a case, both were acting in bad faith. If only one of them was in bad faith, he alone was forbidden to seek the marital right, but he could still accede to the petition of the other spouse, who remained free to seek it.[94]

ARTICLE V. THE CONSEQUENT STATUS OF THE OFFSPRING

The violation of the precept of a legitimate superior who had forbidden the contracting of a marriage gave rise to juridical consequences not only for the consorts but also for their offspring. The

92. Alexander III to the Bishop of Padua: "... donec tamdiu separentur, quousque legitime cognoscatur utrum eorum matrimonium possit et debeat de iure stare." — C. 3, X, *de matrimonio contracto contra interdictum ecclesiae,* IV, 16; Comp. I, c. 5, *de sponsalibus et matrimoniis,* IV, 1; Jaffé, n. 14235; Hostiensis, *Summa Aurea,* tit. *de matrimonio contra interdictum ecclesiae contracto,* p. 317, n. 3.

93. Urbanus III (1185-1187), c. 18, X, *de sponsalibus et matrimoniis,* IV, 1; Comp. I, c. 20, h. t., IV, 1; Jaffé, n. 15729.

94. Hostiensis, *Summa Aurea,* tit. *de matrimonio contra interdictum ecclesiae contracto,* p. 317, n. 3.

children of parents who, when in reality laboring under a diriment impediment, presumed to contract marriage in the face of an ecclesiastical prohibition, were to be considered illegitimate, notwithstanding the ignorance of the parents in regard to the existing diriment impediment.[95]

Although ordinarily the favor of legitimacy was so strong in law that it extended even to children born of an invalid marriage, as long as one of the parties thought the union to be valid,[96] this favor did not apply when the marriage was contracted against the prohibition of the Church. The law presumed that the parents were not in good faith when they thus attempted marriage, for they were held to know about the impediment, or at least to be guilty of affecting ignorance regarding it.[97]

Nor could it be objected that the use of the verb *censeatur* required a previous judicial rendering of a sentence for bringing about this status of illegitimacy. For when a privation was the result, not of the punishment of some delict in the person to be punished, but rather of the lack of some prerequisite condition for the enjoyment of a given privilege, there was no need of a judicial sentence subsequent to the law's acknowledgment of the existing privation.[98]

95. "Si quis vero huiusmodi clandestina vel interdicta coniungia inire praesumpserit, in gradu prohibito etiam ignoranter, soboles de tali coniunctione suscepta, prorsus illegitima censeatur, de parentum ignorantia nullum habitura subsidium." — C. 3, X, *de clandestina desponsatione,* IV, 3.

96. "Nota quod ignorantia alterius parentis facit quod filii de tali matrimonio nati legitimi sunt, et favor prolis ad hoc coadiuvat." — *Glossa Ordinaria,* ad c. 14, X, *qui filii sint legitimi,* IV, 17, s. v. *casus;* "Ex hoc patet quod sufficit bona fides alterius parentis ut filii dicantur legitimi." — *Ibid.,* s. v. *legitimum.*

97. ". . . prorsus illegitima censeatur, de parentum ignorantia nullum habitura subsidium: cum illi taliter contrahendo non expertes scientiae, vel saltem affectatores ignorantiae videantur." — C. 3, X, *de clandestina desponsatione,* IV, 3.

98. Sanchez, *De Matrimonio,* Lib. VII, Disp. VI, n. 9.

Chapter III

HISTORICAL DEVELOPMENT FROM THE COUNCIL OF TRENT TO THE ENACTMENT OF THE CODE OF CANON LAW

During the period from the Council of Trent to the enactment of the Code of Canon Law the matrimonial impediment of personal ban received much greater attention than had previously been accorded it. This was due largely to two factors, namely, to important legislation concerning the impediment, and to a further determination of its nature by canonical writers of the time.

Therefore, before any detailed consideration is given to the various elements of the matrimonial impediment as it existed at the time, it will be helpful to consider its development in general.

Article I. General Developments during This Period

As has been stated, there were two main factors which greatly contributed to the growing importance of this matrimonial impediment during this period. Though in reality these two factors worked together concomitantly, for the purpose of clarity it will be advantageous to treat them separately.

Consideration will accordingly be given first to the legislation and the pronouncements of authority, and secondly to the further determination of the nature of the impediment.

Section 1. *Legislation and Pronouncements of Authority*

With reference to the impediment here in question, the most important legislation is found in the Council of Trent (1545-1563). In a general decree the Church prohibited, under penalty of invalidity, any marriage not contracted before a priest and two witnesses.[1] In

1. Conc. Trident., Sess. XXIV, *de ref. matrim.*, c. 1: "Qui aliter quam praesente parocho, vel alio sacerdote, de ipsius parochi seu ordinarii licentia, et duobus vel tribus testibus matrimonium contrahere attentabunt, eos sancta synodus ad sic contrahendum omnino inhabiles reddit, et hujusmodi contractus irritos et nullos esse decernit, prout eos praesenti decreto irritos facit et annullat." — Mansi, XXXIII, 152.

the same decree it warned temporal lords and magistrates, and forbade them to force their subjects unwillingly into marriages.[2] And lastly, it prohibited the solemnities of marriage during certain periods of the year.[3]

In addition to this legislation of the Council of Trent, there were several decrees of various Roman Congregations which dealt with this impediment. On April 20, 1629, the Sacred Congregation of the Council wrote to the Archbishop of Kiev, Russia, in the name of the Sacred Congregation of the Propagation of the Faith, lauding his zeal in attacking clandestine marriages, but instructing him that only the Supreme Pontiff, the Universal Church, or a General Council can invalidate marriages contracted against their prescriptions,[4] and informing him that the synodal decrees published by him could not invalidate marriages inasmuch as he fundamentally lacked the power to attach such an effect to his decrees, and that consequently the marriages contracted in violation of these decrees were valid as long as no other legitimate impediment was involved.[5]

2. Conc. Trident., Sess. XXIV, *de ref. matrim.*, c. 9: "Quare cum maxime nefarium sit, matrimonii libertatem violare, et ab eis injurias nasci, a quibus jura expectantur, praecipit sancta synodus omnibus, cujuscumque gradus, dignitatis, et conditionis existant, sub anathematis poena, quam ipso facto incurrant, ne quovis modo directe vel indirecte, subditos suos, vel quoscumque alios cogant quo minus libere matrimonia contrahant." — Mansi, XXXIII, 155.

3. Conc. Trident., Sess. XXIV, *de ref. matrim.*, c. 10: "Ab adventu domini nostri Jesu Christi usque in diem epiphaniae, et a feria quarta cinerum usque in octavam paschatis inclusive, antiquas solemnium nuptiarum prohibitiones, diligenter ab omnibus observari sancta synodus praecipit: in aliis vero temporibus nuptias solemniter celebrari permittit, quas episcopi, ut ea qua decet modestia et honestate fiant, curabunt: sancta enim res est matrimonium, et sancte tractandum." — Mansi, XXXIII, 155.

4. "... laudando illius zelum super provisione matrimoniorum clandestinorum, at quia facultas dandi illis formam eaque irritandi reservatur soli Summo Pontifici, seu Ecclesiae Universali, aut Concilio Generali ..." — *Codicis Iuris Canonici Fontes,* cura Emi Petri Card. Gasparri editi (9 vols., Romae [postea Civitate Vaticana]: Typis Polyglottis Vaticanis, 1923-1939 [Vols. VII, VIII, IX, ed. cura et studio Emi Iustiniani Card. Serédi]), n. 2506 (hereafter cited *Fontes*).

5. *Loc. cit.*

Thus, in a negative form, the Sacred Congregation of the Council pointed out the power of the Successor of Peter to prohibit a particular marriage under penalty of invalidity. This same Congregation, in a decree directed to Agrigento on March 15, 1727, reaffirmed this in positive form: it stated that the Pope could prohibit a marriage under penalty of invalidity by specifying an invalidating effect as deriving from a violation of the prohibition.[6] Benedict XIV (1740-1758) reaffirmed this same principle, i. e., marriages contracted in violation of the prohibition of the Supreme Pontiff were null if the prohibition was fortified with the sanction of nullity; otherwise they were valid.[7]

In the decree of March 15, 1727, the Sacred Congregation also pointed out that all prelates subordinate to the Pope were unable to prohibit a marriage under penalty of invalidity, unless their prohibition was founded upon some existing diriment impediment.[8]

---

6. "... licet nonnullis fuerit dubitatum, an matrimonium contractum contra interdictum S. Pontificis sit validum ... vera tamen opinio est, quae adstruit nullitatem matrimonii contra interdictum Papae celebrati, dummodo interdictum fuerit munitum decreto irritante. Sicut etenim Papa potest statuere per legem universalem impedimenta impedientia et dirimentia matrimonium, ita potest in casu particulari sub poena nullitatis interdicere, ne tale matrimonium in casu particulari contrahatur." — *Canones et Decreta Concilii Tridentini, ex Editione Romana a. 1834 Repetiti, Accedunt S. Congr. Card. Conc. Trid. Interpretum Declarationes ac Resolutiones ex ipso Resolutionum Thesauro, et Constitutiones Pontificiae Recentiores ad Ius Commune Spectantes* (Neapoli, 1859), Sess. XXIV. *de reformatione matrimonii,* Sectio N, n. 113, p. 270 (hereafter cited *Canones et Decreta*).

7. "Aliud esset de matrimonio celebrato contra interdictum Papae, munitum decreto irritanti: siquidem, cum Papa possit per suam universalem legem novum impedimentum dirimens matrimonio apponere, potest etiam in aliquo speciali eventu prohibere, ne inter peculiares personas matrimonium contrahatur, simulque decernere, ut contra suam prohibitionem contractum, sit irritum.... Sola vero prohibitio, sine decreto irritante, producit dumtaxat impedimentum impediens, non autem dirimens matrimonium." — Benedictus XIV, *De Synodo Diocesana Libri Tredecim* (4 vols., Mechliniae, 1842), Lib. XII, Cap. V, n. 3.

8. "Et in eo quod attinet ad caeteros praelatos inferiores [praeter Papam], ea recepta videtur esse sententia, ut eorum interdictum non valeat nullitatem matrimonii causare, nisi sit innixum causae perpetuae, hoc est impedimento impedienti et dirimenti, ad differentiam casus, in quo esset innixum causae temporali, hoc est impedimento tantum impedienti." — *Canones et Decreta,* Sess. XXIV, *de ref. matrim.,* Sectio N, n. 113, pp. 269-270.

In accordance with this principle, several decrees of the same Congregation upheld the validity of marriages contracted in violation of the prohibition of the bishop. Thus, for instance, in response to a query of the Bishop of Jaén, Spain, in 1581, the Sacred Congregation replied that in spite of the prohibition by means of which the ordinary forbade the pastor to assist at a certain marriage, the marriage was to be regarded as valid if it was contracted with the assistance either of the pastor or of his delegate.[9]

Again, on April 22, 1719, the Sacred Congregation, in a document sent to the Diocese of Pistoia, upheld the validity of a marriage at which a priest had assisted who was not the pastor but who had received from the vicar general a delegation to assist at the marriage, in spite of the fact that the pastor himself had been forbidden by the bishop to do so.[10]

Another decree of the same Congregation, on February 20, 1723, declared a marriage to be valid although the bishop had forbidden the couple to marry until they obtained a declaration of their freedom in this regard, and they had disregarded his prohibition by marrying without having awaited that declaration.[11]

The Constitution *Dei miseratione* of Benedict XIV, issued on November 3, 1741, emphasized the fact that marriage causes were to be judged by the bishops whenever possible, or at least by those whom the bishops had set up as qualified judges.[12]

Finally, a decree which the Sacred Congregation of the Council issued for the Archdiocese of Florence on February 17, 1629, clearly stated that a bishop could punish those who entered marriage against his prohibition.[13] The Constitution *Dei miseratione* stated that the

---

9. *Canones et Decreta,* Sess. XXIV, *de ref. matrim.,* Sectio N, p. 269, n. 110.

10. *Ibid.,* n. 111.

11. *Ibid.,* n. 112.

12. *Magnum Bullarium Romanum, seu Eiusdem Continuatio* (19 vols., Luxemburgi, 1727-1758), Pars Decima, Tomus XVI, p. 49, n. 4; *Fontes,* n. 318, §4.

13. *Fontes,* n. 2503.

usual penalty imposed on those who contracted marriage against the prohibition of the Church was separation from cohabitation.[14]

This, in brief, reflects the legislation and the pronouncements of authority concerning this matrimonial impediment from the Council of Trent to the enactment of the Code of Canon Law.

SECTION 2. *Further Determination of the Nature of the Impediment*

Having in mind the legislation of the Council of Trent and the pronouncements of authority, the canonical writers of the period proceeded to a more exact determination of the nature of this impediment.

In the first place, they made a distinction between the impediment taken in a wide sense and the impediment taken in a strict sense. In a wide sense any marriage was said to be celebrated contrary to the interdict of the Church when it reflected a disregard of the ecclesiastical sanctions, in that it was attempted or contracted in the face of diriment or prohibiting impediments.[15] It was in this wide sense that under the notion of the Church's interdict Sanchez (1550-1610) included the prescriptions against clandestine marriages and also the sanctions against formless marriages as coming under the matrimonial impediment of personal ban.[16]

However, in a more restricted and proper sense a marriage was said to be celebrated contrary to the interdict of the Church when it was contracted by persons whom a legitimate superior for a just cause had forbidden to do so.[17] It is with the matrimonial impediment in this more restricted sense that the present work is concerned.

---

14. "...quae adversus eos, qui matrimonium contra interdictum ecclesiae contrahunt, statuta sunt, praesertim, ut invicem a cohabitatione separentur." — *Magnum Bullarium Romanum, seu Eiusdem Continuatio,* Pars Decima, Tomus XVI, p. 50, n. 9; *Fontes,* n. 318, §9. Note: This temporary separation was in the nature of a punishment for the violation of an ecclesiastical prohibition. Cf. Chapter III, Article IV, of this historical synopsis.

15. Schmalzgrueber, *Ius Ecclesiasticum Universum* (5 vols. in 12, Romae, 1843-1845), Lib. IV, tit. 16, n. 1.

16. Sanchez, *De Matrimonio,* Lib. VII, Disp. VI, n. 6.

17. Schmalzgrueber, *Ius Ecclesiasticum Universum,* Lib. IV, tit. 16, n. 1; Sanchez, *De Matrimonio,* Lib. VII, Disp. VI, n. 6.

Since the various impedient and diriment impediments have been constituted in the general law for certain definite reasons, one can readily see that for other reasons it could be necessary to prohibit or to invalidate a particular marriage by means of a special precept rather than through a general law; and it is precisely this that is accomplished through the Church's interdict in its more restricted sense.[18]

Taken in this restricted sense, the Church's personal ban relative to the contracting of marriage did in general constitute an impedient impediment. Thus taught Sanchez,[19] Pontius (1569-1629),[20] Fagnanus (1598-1678),[21] and Schmalzgrueber (1663-1735).[22] However, Wernz (1842-1914) added the note that although the Church's ban simply prohibited the marriage, it could also, and did under certain circumstances, invalidate the marriage.[23]

Accordingly, the matrimonial impediment of the Church's personal ban could be defined as a special precept, imposed by a competent ecclesiastical superior for a just cause, by which precept certain persons were either for a time or permanently forbidden to contract a particular marriage, and sometimes were even rendered incapable of doing so.

This, then, was the extent to which this concept had been developed immediately preceding the publication of the Code of Canon Law.

---

18. Wernz, *Ius Decretalium,* Tom. IV, *Ius Matrimoniale* (Romae, 1904), n. 593 (hereafter cited *Ius Matrimoniale*).

19. "Et hoc interdictum impediet matrimonium licite contrahi, non tamen dirimet." — *De Matrimonio,* Lib. VII, Disp. VI, n. 6.

20. "Interdictum quidem impedit contrahere matrimonium ex communi certaque sententia." — *De Sacramento Matrimonii Tractatus,* Lib. VI, Cap. VII, p. 227, n. 1.

21. "Nota matrimonium contra interdictum ecclesiae, vel judicis contractum, nisi aliud obsistat canonicum impedimentum non esse irritum, separatio enim conjugum hic non fit quoad foedus matrimonii, sed quoad thorum donec causa interdicti cognoscatur." — Fagnanus, *Commentaria,* Lib. IV, tit. *de matrimonio contracto contra interdictum ecclesiae,* p. 76, n. 4.

22. "In hoc secundo sensu acceptum interdictum constituit speciale impedimentum, non dirimens, sed impediens matrimonium." — Schmalzgrueber, *Ius Ecclesiasticum Universum,* Lib. IV, tit. 16, n. 1.

23. Wernz, *Ius Matrimoniale,* n. 594.

ARTICLE II. THE AUTHOR OF THE BAN

This impediment derived from the special precept imposed by a competent ecclesiastical superior. Thus it derived *ab homine* rather than *a iure.* The reader's interest will accordingly center on the various Church authorities who were capable of exercising such prohibitive power.

SECTION 1. *The Supreme Pontiff*

Although it was commonly agreed that in general the Church's ban of marriage constituted an impedient impediment and therefore did not invalidate a marriage contracted in contravention of its precept, it was not at all certain that such was the case if the prohibition was imposed by the Holy Father. In the case of prelates other than the Supreme Pontiff, there was no uncertainty. In the early days of the Church, it is true, bishops had been granted the faculty by law of establishing diriment impediments.[24] But beyond doubt this was not the case subsequent to the Council of Trent. The ban, when issued by prelates other than the Roman Pontiff, was incapable of invalidating a marriage.[25]

As far as the Supreme Pontiff himself was concerned, all were agreed that he could prohibit any of the faithful in the Universal Church from contracting a particular marriage, for he was the supreme pastor and judge of all Christians throughout the whole world.[26] But the fact that several decrees seemed expressly to be mutually contradictory still gave rise to doubts and disagreement about the ability of the Supreme Pontiff to impose a precept which would render a marriage invalid.

For instance, there were two texts which seemed to state that marriages contracted in violation of the interdict of the Church were

24. Pontius, *De Sacramento Matrimonii Tractatus,* Lib. VI, Cap. VII, p. 227, n. 2.

25. Sanchez, *De Matrimonio,* Lib. VII, Disp. II, n. 2.

26. Wernz, *Ius Matrimoniale,* n. 597; Schmalzgrueber, *Ius Ecclesiasticum Universum,* Lib. IV, tit. 16, n. 3.

invalid. One of these read as follows: "Si contra interdictum ecclesiae publice factum venire praesumpserit, contractum poteris irritare."[27] A similar text stated: "Quod si contra interdictum nostrum in praeiudicium ipsius aliquid fuerit attentatum, id irritum esse decernimus, et viribus omnino carere."[28] A third text contained these words: "Nam quod contra interdictum et ordinem Ecclesiae factum est, ratum non haberi, tam divinae quam humanae legis proclamat auctoritas."[29]

On the other hand, the decretals which treated explicitly of the matrimonial impediment here under discussion carried a wording that was in direct opposition to the texts just cited. For instance, Book IV, Title XVI, Chapter 2, of the Decretals read as follows:

> Licet enim contra interdictum ecclesiae ad secunda vota transire non debuerit, non est tamen conveniens, ut ob id solum sacramentum coniugii dissolvatur. Aliqua tamen poenitentia eis debet imponi, qui contra prohibitionem ecclesiae hoc fecerunt.[30]

As a result of the apparent contradiction of these various texts, there was in some quarters doubt as to whether the Roman Pontiff could impose a precept which would render a marriage invalid. It was generally admitted that for a just cause he could impose a general law which would invalidate a marriage between certain classes (*genera*) of people. But some were not so certain that in an analogous manner, and for a similar just cause, he could prohibit marriage between private individuals in such a way that the marriage would be null if an attempt were made to violate the prohibition.

Thus Martinus de Azpilcueta (Navarrus) (1493-1586), though he raised the question, did not come to any conclusion; he merely

---

27. C. 4, X, *de sponsa duorum,* IV, 4; Comp. I, c. 9, h. t., IV, 4; Jaffé, n. 13969.

28. C. 13, X, *de desponsatione impuberum,* IV, 2; Comp. III, c. 1, h. t., IV, 2; Potthast, n. 535.

29. C. 2, C. XXXV, q. 6; Jaffé, n. 384.

30. C. 2, X, *de iis qui contrahunt matrimonium contra interdictum ecclesiae,* IV, 16.

stated that it would not be expedient for the Pope to do so.[31] He admitted, however, that the Pope would be able to prohibit a marriage, and also to forbid the pastor to assist at it, but affirmed that the marriage would be valid if nevertheless it was contracted against such a papal prohibition.[32] He stated that he had never heard of any Pope attempting to impose an invalidating precept, and that even if the Pope could do so, it was not expedient for him to exercise such power.[33] Thus Navarrus chose not to be definitive on the matter of whether the Pope could impose a truly invalidating precept.

Sanchez, however, spoke much more to the point. He stated that when there was a just cause the Supreme Pontiff was certainly capable of imposing an invalidating precept in a particular case forbidding certain private individuals to contract marriage.[34] Sanchez argued that if the Pope possessed the power to invalidate marriage between all persons of a certain type (*generis*) for a just cause, he certainly also had the power to do the same thing in the case of certain private individuals when an equally urgent cause demanded it.

In general, commentators were inclined to agree with Sanchez on the main principle, namely, that under certain circumstances the Roman Pontiff could impose a precept which rendered any marriage contracted in contravention of it invalid.[35] However, they disagreed on the cir-

---

31. Navarrus, *Consiliorum seu Responsorum Tomus Alter* (Venetiis, 1621), Lib. IV, tit. *de matrimonio contracto contra interdictum ecclesiae,* Consilium I, n. 2.

32. "Respondeo primo, certum esse circa hanc quaestionem, quod Papa summus Christi Vicarius potest iusta de causa matrimonium interdicere alicui usque ad aliquod tempus, ut satis probat totus titulus. Secundo, huiusmodi interdictum inducere quidem impedimentum impediens matrimonium contrahendum, sed non dirimens post contractum." —*Ibid.,* n. 1.

33. "Quarto, rem sine exemplo esse, quod Papa per suum interdictum particulare duas personas alioquin habiles faciat inhabiles ad contrahendum inter se matrimonium, ita ut contractum sit nullum, et ita mea sententia indignam, quae petatur, et indigniorem, quae concedatur, cui consequens est, praedictum motum proprium non debere peti, neque concedi." —*Ibid.,* n. 2.

34. Sanchez, *De Matrimonio,* Lib. VII, Disp. I, n. 7.

35. Fagnanus, *Commentaria,* Lib. IV, tit. *de matrimonio contracto contra interdictum ecclesiae,* p. 76, n. 7.

cumstances and conditions under which the precept would have this effect.

The solutions proposed by the writers were both numerous and varied.[36] The correct solution seems to be the one proposed by Pontius. If the prohibition relative to a future marriage did not contain an invalidating clause, then the marriage was to be regarded as valid even if contracted contrary to the prohibition.[37] This doctrine Pontius proposed as the common opinion of his day,[38] and as the decision contained in the appendix of the III Lateran Council held under Alexander III:

> Licet enim contra interdictum ecclesiae ad secunda vota transire nequaquam debuerit, conveniens non videtur ut ob id solum Sacramentum coniugii dissolvatur. Alia enim poena debebit eis imponi, quod contra prohibitionem ecclesiae hoc fecerunt.[39]

For marriage was a holy state, and the dissolution of the bond was a very serious matter, not to be taken lightly. Therefore the invalidity of a marriage was not to be regarded as resulting from a mere prohibition.

Moreover, such was the case whether the pontifical prohibition was given in the form of a constitution or of a precept. For the form

---

36. Cf. Emmanuel Gonzalez-Tellez, *Commentaria Perpetua in Singulos Textus Quinque Librorum Decretalium Gregorii IX* (5 vols., Lugduni, 1673), Lib. IV, Tit. XVI, c. 3, n. 2; Sanchez, *De Matrimonio,* Lib. VII, Disp. II, nn. 3, 4, 5, 7; *Glossa Ordinaria,* ad c. 4, X, *de sponsa duorum,* IV, 4, s. v. *poteris irritare; Glossa Ordinaria,* ad c. 13, X, *de desponsatione impuberum,* IV, 2, s. v. *irritum.*

37. Pontius, *De Sacramento Matrimonii Tractatus,* Lib. VI, Cap. VII, p. 228, n. 3.

38. *Loc. cit.* Cf. also Augustinus Barbosa, *Collectanea Doctorum tam Veterum quam Recentiorum in Ius Pontificium Universum* (5 vols., Lugduni, 1656), Lib. IV, Tit. XVI, c. 2, n. 1: "Collige ex texto non esse irritum matrimonium si contra prohibitionem temporalem Pontificium illud ineatur"; Fagnanus, *Commentaria,* Lib. IV, tit. *de matrimonio contracto contra interdictum ecclesiae,* p. 76, n. 8: "Matrimonium contractum contra interdictum Papae mero iure tenet, alio impedimento non extante."

39. Cap. XXVIII, Mansi, XXII, 296. Cf. c. 2, X, *de matrimonio contracto contra interdictum ecclesiae,* IV, 16, where this text occurs.

in which the prohibition was made exercised no effect upon the subsequent validity or invalidity of the marriage.[40] Nor did it matter whether the cause of the prohibition was temporary or perpetual. For a simple prohibition, whether temporary or perpetual, did not invalidate what otherwise was valid.[41]

But if an invalidating clause was included in the prohibition, then a marriage attempted in contravention of the prohibition was invalid. And this applied whether the cause was temporary or perpetual, or whether the invalidating clause was stated in general or was referred to marriage in particular.[42]

Schmalzgrueber[43] further explained that there was an essential difference between prohibiting and invalidating. Accordingly, the nullity of a marriage was not to be inferred from the fact that the marriage was prohibited, for it was a well-known rule of law that many things were prohibited which yet obtained the sanction of the law once they had actually been performed.[44] However, if a nullifying clause was added, then a marriage contracted in contravention of the prohibition was null.

It made no difference whether such a prohibition was imposed in the form of a general constitution or of a personal precept. For a prohibition imposed by means of a general constitution differed from an interdict imposed by means of a personal precept only in its extension, but not in its obligating power or invalidating effect.

Likewise, it made little if any difference whether the invalidating decree was general or particular in its form, for in either case it produced its effect of invalidating the prohibited act.[45]

Wernz summed up the matter as follows: Only the Roman Pontiff is able to add to his prohibition an invalidating decree. And even the prohibition of the Supreme Pontiff does not produce this invalidating

---

40. Pontius, *De Sacramento Matrimonii Tractatus*, Lib. VI, Cap. VII, p. 228, n. 4.

41. *Loc. cit.*

42. *Ibid.*, n. 5.

43. *Ius Ecclesiasticum Universum*, Lib. IV, tit. 16, n. 10.

44. C. 16, X, *de regularibus et transeuntibus ad religionem*, III, 31.

45. Schmalzgrueber, *Ius Ecclesiasticum Universum*, Lib. IV, tit. 16, n. 11.

effect unless it is clearly stated in the prohibition that such is the intention of its author. Otherwise the decree remains a mere prohibition, which makes a marriage illicit but not invalid.[46]

Sanchez raised one further question: whether it was within the power of the Pope to render a person perpetually incapable of contracting matrimony. This case differs from the case previously discussed insofar as in that instance those who were rendered incapable of marrying each other were not, by that fact, restricted to living a life of celibacy. They were left free to marry others if they so desired. The question, as Sanchez proposed it, regarded the ability of the Roman Pontiff to command a person to live a life of celibacy, and to deprive him of the right to marriage, which had been established and existed as a remedy for concupiscence.

Sanchez cited the fact that Pope Urban V rendered Bernabò Visconti (1323-1385) and his sons incapable of contracting marriage because they were rebels against the Church.[47] Sanchez believed that such an action really was within the competence of the Supreme Pontiff, and cited Calderinus († 1365) and Alexander de Nevo († ca. 1483) as having supported the same view.[48] He argued that, although everyone had from the very law of nature a right to marry, nevertheless the Supreme Pontiff was able to deprive a person of that right as a punishment for an exceptionally grave delict. If the Pope was able to prohibit marriage perpetually to a person as a punishment for a crime committed, and could do this in such a way that the person could not marry without grave sin, then, Sanchez argued, when the gravity of the delict warranted it, the Pope could prohibit marriage perpetually in such a way that an attempt to violate this prohibition would result in an invalid marriage. For the pontifical power in regard to the sacrament of marriage was not restricted to the imposing of impedient impediments only, but extended to the imposing of diriment impediments as well.[49]

46. *Ius Matrimoniale,* n. 602.

47. "Urbanum V reddidisse inhabiles ad matrimonium ineundum Barnahovem Vicecomitem et dominum Mediolanensem, ac liberos eius rebelles ecclesiae." — Sanchez, *De Matrimonio,* Lib. VII, Disp. I, n. 8.

48. *Loc. cit.*

49. *Loc. cit.*

SECTION 2. *The Local Bishop*

In regard to the local bishop, Sanchez was of the opinion that from the exclusive viewpoint of the divine law, whether positive or natural, it was within the radical power of the local bishop to establish diriment impediments for his own diocese, just as it was within the power of the Supreme Pontiff to establish diriment impediments for the Church at large. For he claimed that whatever the Pope could do in and for the Church universally, the bishop could do in and for his own diocese, unless the Pope had reserved the right to himself.[50] However, Sanchez readily admitted that the bishop could no longer establish diriment impediments, for in his opinion the Pope had reserved this right to himself. And since he could not find any specific ruling by which this reservation had been effected, Sanchez concluded that the reservation must have derived from the general practice of the Church.[51]

Regardless of the truth or falsity of Sanchez' opinion as to why it was so, it was certain that the bishop could not establish a diriment impediment, even in his own diocese.[52] Thus Benedict XIV in his *De Synodo Diocesana* stated that it was not within the power of the bishop to set up a new diriment impediment, since this could be done solely by the Supreme Pontiff. It was for this reason that the Sacred Congregation of the Council honored as valid a marriage which had been celebrated before a pastor whom the bishop had forbidden to assist at marriages. For the prohibition of the bishop affected merely the lawfulness of the pastor's assistance at the marriage, and not its validity.[53]

---

50. Sanchez, *De Matrimonio,* Lib. VII, Disp. I, n. 9.

51. *Loc. cit.*

52. Fagnanus, *Commentaria,* Lib. IV, tit. *de matrimonio contracto contra interdictum ecclesiae,* p. 76, n. 10.

53. "... neque in Episcopi potestate est, novum statuere impedimentum dirimens, quod a solo Summo Pontifice potest induci.... Quocirca eadem Sacra Congregatio concilii ... validum definivit matrimonium celebratum coram Parocho, cui ab episcopo sit generatim interdictum, ne matrimoniis assistat: 'Congregatio Cardinalium respondit valere matrimonium contractum coram parocho, cui interdictum est ab Episcopo, ne interveniat.' ... Prohibitio autem Episcopi solum operatur, ne ille Parochus licite, non itidem ne valide assistat." — Benedictus XIV, *De Synodo Diocesana,* Lib. XII, Cap. V, n. 2.

In the same work Benedict XIV cited two responses of the Sacred Congregation of the Council to the Bishop of Jaén, in 1581 — both of which upheld the validity of a marriage contracted in violation of the prohibition of the bishop.[54] In addition he made the following declaration:

> Cum enim ea non sit episcopo auctoritas, ut possit inducere impedimentum dirimens, quod non est, aut aliquod matrimonium, quod ex canonum praescripto nullum irritumque non sit, nullum irritumque statuere; illicitum quidem erit matrimonium, si celebretur coram eo, cui episcopus huiusmodi celebrationi adesse vetuerit; graviter etiam peccabit is, qui spreta superioris prohibitione, eidem assistentiam praebebit; at nulla ratione dici poterit, matrimonium ipsum nullitatis vitio subiacere.[55]

In accordance with this principle, Wernz stated that the bishop lacked the power of appending an invalidating clause;[56] and Schmalzgrueber taught that this was the common opinion of the authorities, for since prelates inferior to the Pope did not have the power to institute invalidating matrimonial impediments, their prohibition could not affect the validity of a marriage.[57]

However, without doubt it was within the competence of the bishop to prohibit a particular marriage in his own diocese.[58] His

---

54. "Valere matrimonium contractum coram parocho, cui interdictum est ab episcopo ne interveniat." "Utrum matrimonium in quo intervenerit Vicarius Parochi, non invitus, sed volens, contra prohibitionem tantum ordinarii, sit validum, vel potius invalidum, quia non intervenit sacerdos habens iurisdictionem, cum sit sublata ab ordinario? — Esse validum." — Benedictus XIV, *De Synodo Dioecesana,* Lib. XIII, Cap. XXIII, n. 1.

55. *Ibid.,* n. 3.

56. ". . . sed potestate apponendi clausulam irritantem episcopus caret." — *Ius Matrimoniale,* n. 601.

57. "Ratio est, qui cum huiusmodi praelati [Papae inferiores] non habeant potestatem statuendi impedimenta nuptialia dirimentia matrimonium, ipsorum prohibitio istius valori obstare non potest." — *Ius Ecclesiasticum Universum,* Lib. IV, tit. 16, n. 8.

58. "Determinatum quoddam matrimonium inter certas personas contrahendum per praeceptum vetari potest ab episcopo." — Wernz, *Ius Matrimoniale,* n. 597. "Quaeritur quis superior ex huiusmodi causa interdicere matrimonium possit? Certum est idem posse episcopum respectu suae dioecesis." — Schmalzgrueber, *Ius Ecclesiasticum Universum,* Lib. IV, tit. 16, n. 3.

power in this matter extended not only to the spouses themselves but also to the pastor and the witnesses. For the bishop could prohibit the assistance of the pastor and of the witnesses expressly and under the threat of grave penalties to be inflicted at his discretion.[59] But, as has been noted, if the pastor and witnesses nevertheless did assist at the marriage, this prohibition had no effect upon its validity.[60]

Although the prohibition of the bishop did not affect the validity of the marriage in question, it did, in general, impose a grave obligation regarding the non-celebration of the marriage.[61] The only exceptions to this rule obtained when the prohibition had been imposed for some rather trifling reason, or when the spouses themselves knew with certainty that the suspicion regarding the presence of an impediment had no foundation, and that accordingly there was no danger of the emergence of scandal from the celebration of the marriage.[62]

Moreover, it was within the power of the bishop to punish those who violated his prohibition. Thus Schmalzgrueber pointed out that, lest the prohibition be treated with contempt for lack of binding force, it was within the power of the bishop to separate for a time spouses who had violated his prohibition, and to impose on them a suitable penance.[63] The determining of the duration of the time of separation was left to the discretion of the bishop.[64] If he deemed it advisable, the bishop could impose some other suitable penance in place of the separation, and this was always to be done if otherwise there would result for the parties the danger of incontinence.[65]

However, the fact remained that it was within the bishop's power to impose very severe penalties for the violation of his prohibition in regard to marriage, for the penalties were not specified in the law, but the determining of them was left to his own prudent judgment.[66]

---

59. Wernz, *Ius Matrimoniale*, n. 598.
60. *Loc. cit.*
61. *Ibid.*, n. 601.
62. *Loc. cit.*
63. *Ius Ecclesiasticum Universum*, Lib. IV, tit. 16, n. 8.
64. *Loc. cit.*
65. *Loc. cit.*
66. Benedictus XIV, *De Synodo Diocesana*, Lib. XII, Cap. V, n. 4; Sanchez, *De Matrimonio*, Lib. III, Disp. XLVI, n. 7.

The Sacred Congregation of the Council explicitly declared that it was within his power even to impose monetary fines, provided that the receipts of these were applied to works of piety.[67] All this, of course, presumed that in exercising his power the bishop was careful not to abuse his authority or to infringe upon the common law.[68]

Although in this matter the consideration has turned primarily upon the local bishop, it is certain that this same power belonged to other ecclesiastical prelates who enjoyed quasi-episcopal power over the clergy and people of a certain territory.[69] Thus this same power belonged to the prelate *nullius*, the vicar apostolic, the vicar capitular (administrator), and the vicar general over their own subjects.[70] Moreover, it was also within the competence of the ecclesiastical judge to impose this prohibition, for it was his duty to decide matrimonial causes and to take all necessary precautions for the protection of this august sacrament.[71]

SECTION 3. *The Parish Priest*

Not only were the Pope and the bishop competent to prohibit a particular marriage, but this same power belonged also to the pastor.[72] In this regard Sanchez explained that the pastor had the power to prohibit a particular marriage but was not entitled to render a decision concerning the reason for his prohibition.[73] Wernz contended that through such a prohibitory precept the pastor did not usurp the jurisdiction of the external forum or the office of the matrimonial judge, but merely imposed a temporary prohibition in a matter of

---

67. S. C. C., *Florentina,* 17 febr. 1629, ad 5: Q. "An possit in eisdem casibus punire poenis pecuniariis, locis tamen piis applicandis? R. Posse." — *Pontes,* n. 2503.

68. Benedictus XIV, *De Synodo Diocesana,* Lib. XII, Cap. V, n. 4.

69. Schmalzgrueber, *Ius Ecclesiasticum Universum,* Lib. IV, tit. 16, n. 3.

70. Wernz, *Ius Matrimoniale,* n. 597.

71. Schmalzgrueber, *Ius Ecclesiasticum Universum,* Lib. IV, tit. 16, n. 4; Sanchez, *De Matrimonio,* Lib. VII, Disp. VI, n. 6.

72. Pontius, *De Sacramento Matrimonii Tractatus,* Lib. VI, Cap. VII, p. 227, n. 2; Sanchez, *De Matrimonio,* Lib. VII, Disp. VI, n. 6.

73. Sanchez, *De Matrimonio,* Lib. III, Disp. XV, n. 3.

discipline that rested under his control.[74] When the freedom of the parties remained in doubt, it was the local pastor's duty to forbid the marriage until the doubt was favorably resolved by the ordinary ecclesiastical judge.[75]

It is to be noted, therefore, that this prohibitory act on the part of the pastor was not one of judicial jurisdiction, for the pastor did not have any right to act as judge or to issue a judicial decree.[76] It was for this reason that the pastor was said to issue the prohibition *extrajudicially.* There was an essential difference between prohibitions which were issued judicially and those issued extrajudicially. A judicial prohibition in the form of a sentence implied and necessarily presupposed a judicial hearing and the settlement of the cause as heard in court. On the other hand, a simple prohibition did not involve a judicial inquiry, and much less implied any ultimate settlement.

Wernz described this authority of the pastor in the external forum as an economic or domestic authority over the parish, which should be considered as an imperfect society. He claimed that pastors participated in the public magisterium of the Church and exercised a certain voluntary jurisdiction in the external forum.[77] Therefore, although a pastor was not able to adjudicate a matrimonial cause, it was still within his power to prohibit a marriage extrajudicially until the competent judge had rendered a judicial decision.[78]

Thus, even though there was a founded suspicion of the presence of some impediment, the pastor did not make any decision concerning

---

74. Wernz, *Ius Matrimoniale,* n. 597.

75. Schmalzgrueber, *Ius Ecclesiasticum Universum,* Lib. IV, tit. 16, n. 5.

76. Fagnanus, *Commentaria,* Lib. IV, tit. *de matrimonio contracto contra interdictum ecclesiae,* p. 76, n. 12.

77. Wernz, *Ius Decretalium,* Tom. II (Romae, 1899), tit. 39, n. 828: "Nam parochi *ex officio externa* et *publica* possunt dare *praecepta* (vetitum matrimonii) aut investigare (in examine sponsorum de impedimentis) aut moderate coercere discolos; item ex missione canonica exercent *publicum* magisterium et iurisdictionem quandam *voluntariam.* Ergo potestas parochorum licet vera perfectaque iurisdictio fori *externi* non sit, tamen est potestas quaedam *oeconomica* vel domestica in parochiam ut societatem *imperfectam,* quae praeter iurisdictionem fori poenitentialis *administrationem* quoque vere *externam* habet adnexam."

78. Schmalzgrueber, *Ius Ecclesiasticum Universum,* Lib. IV, tit. 16, n. 6.

this impediment when he issued his prohibition. For since he lacked judicial power, it was not within his competence to render a decision concerning the impediment; he merely forbade the parties to marry until a decision had been rendered by the competent authority.[79]

Moreover, the violation of this parochial prohibition by the parties concerned did not of itself nullify the marriage. For the pastor was without any power to render anyone incapable of contracting marriage. Therefore, unless some diriment impediment was involved, a marriage contracted in violation of the prohibition of the pastor was valid but illicit.[80]

Yet, as has been said, the pastor did possess, as part of his paternal authority, the power to impede certain marriages.[81] Wernz referred to this power with his use of the expression *"vetitum matrimoniale,"* and he regarded it as part of the pastor's disciplinary authority.[82] And long before the time of Wernz it had been pointed out by Böckhn (1690-1752) that despite the pastor's lack of perfect jurisdiction in the external forum, his obligation of impeding particular marriages clearly formed a part of his general obligation of invoking effective means against the emergence of scandals and vices within the confines of his spiritual jurisdiction.[83]

Thus, when the circumstances warranted it, the pastor could impose his prohibition under penalty of serious sin, that is, he could impose upon the parties concerned a grave obligation of not marrying until their cause had been adjudicated by a competent judge.[84] This applied

79. Sanchez, *De Matrimonio,* Lib. III, Disp. XV, n. 3.

80. Pontius, *De Sacramento Matrimonii Tractatus,* Lib. VI, Cap. VII, p. 227, n. 2.

81. Sanchez, *De Matrimonio,* Lib. VII, Disp. VI, n. 6.

82. Wernz, *Ius Decretalium,* Tom. II, tit. 39, n. 828.

83. Böckhn, *Commentarius in Ius Canonicum Universum* (Salisburgi, et invenitur Parisiis, 1776), Lib. IV, tit. XVI, n. 2; cf. also Schmier, *Jurisprudentia Canonico-Civilis seu Ius Canonicum Universum* (2 vols., Venetiis, 1754), Lib. IV, Tract. III, Cap. 1, n. 79: "... Tametsi parocho non competat jurisdictio fori externi, vel judicialis cognitio causarum matrimonialium, extrajudicialiter tamen in impedimenta matrimonii inquirere, et ad peccatum impediendum, nonnullis personis matrimonium interdicere non prohibetur."

84. Wernz, *Ius Matrimoniale,* n. 600.

only in the presence of some grave danger of serious sin if the prohibition was violated. When the prohibition was imposed for a less serious reason, or when the spouses themselves had certain knowledge that the suspicion of the existence of some impediment was without foundation, the violation of the prohibition did not involve a serious sin.[85]

The authority of the pastor in issuing this prohibition extended to his assistants and to the witnesses as well as to the parties directly concerned.[86] In this regard it is to be noted that if the assistant had not received delegation directly from the bishop to assist at all marriages, he could not validly assist at marriages without a special delegation granted by the pastor in each individual case. Therefore, under such circumstances — when the pastor had forbidden the assistant to assist at a particular marriage — the assistant's violation of the parochial prohibition rendered the marriage not only illicit but even invalid.[87]

ARTICLE III. CAUSES FOR THE ISSUANCE OF A VALID BAN

Inasmuch as the denial — even though only for a time — of the right to marriage in a particular instance entailed a serious infringement upon a man's natural rights, the imposition of a precept in this matter required a just cause. In fact, if the precept was imposed without a just cause, it was null and void in its effect.[88]

The causes which justified bishops and pastors in prohibiting marriages in specific instances could fundamentally be reduced to three: (1) A complaint because of previous espousals entered into with a third party at the instance of the party injured; (2) the founded suspicion of the presence of a latent impediment, whether

85. *Ibid.*, in nota.

86. *Ibid.*, n. 598.

87. *Loc. cit.*

88. "... aut interdictum fit sine causa, et tunc nullum est interdictum." — Hostiensis, *Summa Aurea,* tit. *de matrimonio contra interdictum ecclesiae contracto,* p. 317, n. 3

diriment or prohibitive; (3) the probable conjecture of the emergence of serious quarrels, enmities, or scandal[89] from the marriage.[90]

Even when the Supreme Pontiff intervened there had to be a just cause for the licit imposition of a matrimonial impediment. For the pontifical power was to be used, not indiscriminately, but only in the interests of the right administration of the Church. This demanded that such a fundamental natural right as the contracting of marriage should not be denied except for a just cause. And since a more serious reason was needed to justify the Supreme Pontiff in invalidating a marriage than to justify him in prohibiting the same, it often happened that there existed a sufficient cause for him to prohibit a marriage, though the existing cause proved insufficient to justify the addition of an invalidating clause.[91]

There naturally arose the question whether the prohibition of the Roman Pontiff was of valid effect if it was imposed without a just cause. In other words, if the pontifical prohibition was not founded on a just cause, did it render a marriage contracted in violation of it sinful in the case of a mere prohibition, and invalid in the case of a prohibition which contained an invalidating clause? Sanchez contended that a just cause was necessary for the validity of the prohibition. Therefore, when such a cause did not exist, a marriage contracted in contravention of a pontifical prohibition was both valid and licit.[92]

Wernz pointed out that although the Pope was not so rigorously bound to the causes expressed in law as were the bishops and pastors, nevertheless the Supreme Pontiff used his power rarely and with great moderation.[93] Usually he did so only in connection with certain

---

89. Cf. pp. 99-102 of the present work for a more complete treatment of the post-Tridentine and pre-Code doctrine relative to scandal as a cause for the prohibition.

90. Schmalzgrueber, *Ius Ecclesiasticum Universum,* Lib. IV, tit. 16, n. 2; Wernz, *Ius Matrimoniale,* n. 599.

91. Sanchez, *De Matrimonio,* Lib. VII, Disp. I, n. 4.

92. "Caeterum omnino tenendum est ad valorem prohibitionis desiderari justam causam. Et proinde ea non existente, dicendum est matrimonium contra eum initum, validum esse, et culpa vacare." — Sanchez, *De Matrimonio,* Lib. VII, Disp. I, n. 6.

93. Wernz, *Ius Matrimoniale,* n. 599.

dispensations. Thus, in dispensations from the impediment of a vow, there usually was attached a clause which stated that the spouse who outlived the union could not again contract a marriage. Or in dispensations *"super rato et non consummato"* which involved a serious doubt about the impotence of one of the parties, the dispensation was usually accompanied with a mandate imposed on the doubtfully impotent consort: "Vetito mulieri (viro) transitu ad alias nuptias inconsulta S. Congregatione."[94]

If the prohibition had been imposed by a bishop or by a pastor, then anyone who felt that an injustice had been done because the prohibition was imposed without a sufficient cause could invoke a recourse to a superior authority, that is, to the metropolitan, or to the Sacred Congregation of the Council.[95] Such appeals actually were made — some of them with gratifying results from the viewpoint of the plaintiff.

Thus, at the instance of the mother of one of the spouses, a vicar general prohibited a certain couple from marrying, under threat of excommunication if the prohibition were violated. Recourse was interposed with the Holy See, and the Sacred Congregation of the Council decided that the marriage was to be permitted.[96]

Again, at the instance of relatives, a certain count was forbidden to marry on the twofold ground of disparity of age and probable impotence. When the Sacred Congregation of the Council was consulted, it declared that his marriage was not to be impeded.[97]

In still another case, a certain baroness petitioned the diocesan court to forbid the marriage of her son. The court dismissed the plea as unwarranted. The baroness appealed to Rome. Meanwhile,

---

94. S. C. C., *Calven. et Theanen.,* 18 dec. 1869: "Vetito mulieri transitu ad alias nuptias inconsulta S. Congregatione." — *Fontes,* n. 4216; S. C. C., 15 dec. 1877: "Comiti Z. non liceat transire ad alias nuptias, nisi petita prius et obtenta venia ab apostolica Sede." — *Acta Sanctae Sedis* (41 vols., Romae, 1865-1908), XI (1878), 141 (hereafter cited *ASS*); S. C. C., dec. 1883: "Vetito viro transitu ad alias nuptias, inconsulta S. Congregatione." — *ASS,* XVIII (1885), 409.

95. Wernz, *Ius Matrimoniale,* n. 599.

96. S. C. C., *Florentina,* 12 ian. 1726 — *Canones et Decreta,* p. 270, n. 115.

97. S. C. C., *Tridentina,* 7 sept. 1793 — *Ibid.,* p. 271, n. 118.

the son presented a petition asking that he be allowed to marry even though the appeal of his mother in this regard was still pending. The Sacred Congregation of the Council (July 9, 1881) confirmed the decision of the diocesan court by permitting him to marry.[98]

ARTICLE IV. EFFECTS CONSEQUENT UPON THE VIOLATION OF A VALID BAN

SECTION 1. *Penalties Incurred by the Contracting Parties*

Although the marriage contracted in violation of a prohibition was valid (except in the case of a pontifical prohibition accompanied with an invalidating clause), nevertheless, when the prohibition itself was legitimate, the parties were to be temporarily separated as a punishment for their violation of the ecclesiastical prohibition. This measure was employed for the purpose of deterring the parties from violating the prohibition on the grounds that it lacked a penal sanction.[99] The determining of the duration of the period of separation was left to the discretion of the one who imposed the penalty.[100]

Since the separation was to serve as a punishment for the violation of an ecclesiastical prohibition, the Church desired that only the guilty party be inconvenienced by it. Therefore, if only one of the parties was guilty of knowingly violating the prohibition, that party alone was forbidden to seek the *"debitum,"* but there remained the obligation to render the *"debitum"* at the request of the other partner. On the other hand, if both parties knowingly had violated the prohibition, then the use of marriage was completely forbidden to both during the period of separation.[101]

It was within the competence of the authority which imposed the penance to prescribe also other forms than that of the separation

98. *ASS,* XIV (1881), 455 sq.

99. Sanchez, *De Matrimonio,* Lib. VII, Disp. II, n. 14; Pontius, *De Sacramento Matrimonii Tractatus,* Lib. VI, Cap. VII, p. 228, n. 7; Fagnanus, *Commentaria,* Lib. IV, tit. *de matrimonio contracto contra interdictum ecclesiae,* p. 76, n. 1 and n. 4.

100. Schmalzgrueber, *Ius Ecclesiasticum Universum,* Lib. IV, tit. 16, n. 8; Pontius, *De Sacramento Matrimonii Tractatus,* Lib. VI, Cap. VII, p. 228, n. 7.

101. Sanchez, *loc. cit.;* Pontius, *loc. cit.*

of the parties if this were desirable.[102] In fact, the penalty of separation was always to be commuted to some other form of penance whenever there was danger of incontinence on the part of the spouses concerned.[103]

SECTION 2. *Consequent Status of the Offspring*

If a marriage contracted in violation of an ecclesiastical prohibition subsequently was found to be invalid, then the children of such a marriage were to be considered illegitimate, notwithstanding the ignorance of the parents in regard to the presence of the diriment impediment. This was especially true if the proclamation of the banns had been omitted, or if the marriage had been prohibited because of some doubt that pointed to the likely presence of a diriment impediment.[104] In such a case neither party could be presumed to be in good faith.[105]

It is true that the favor of legitimacy was so strong in law that the children were honored as legitimate even when they were born of an invalid marriage, provided only that both parties, or even one of the parties, thought the union to be valid.[106]

But this rule did not apply in cases of clandestine marriage, or when marriage was contracted against the prohibition of the Church. In these cases, precisely because of the nonobservance of the caution prescribed by the law, the alleged good faith of the parents was not of any avail to the offspring.[107] The law presumed that parents were

---

102. Schmalzgrueber, *loc. cit.*

103. Sanchez, *loc. cit.;* Pontius, *loc. cit.;* Schmalzgrueber, *loc. cit.*

104. Wernz, *Ius Matrimoniale,* n. 603.

105. *Loc. cit.*

106. "Nota quod ignorantia alterius parentis facit quod filii de tali matrimonio nati legitimi sunt, et favor prolis ad hoc coadjuvat." — *Glossa Ordinaria,* ad c. 14, X, *qui filii sint legitimi,* IV, 17, s. v. *casus;* "Ex hoc patet, quod sufficit bona fides alterius parentis, ut filii dicantur legitimi." — *Ibid.,* s. v. *legitimum.*

107. Santi, *Praelectiones Iuris Canonici* (5 vols. in 2, Ratisbonae, Neo Eboraci, et Cincinnati, 1886), Lib. IV, Tit. XVII, n. 3.

not acting in good faith when they thus attempted marriage, for they were held to know about the impediment, or at least to be guilty of affecting ignorance regarding it.[108]

ARTICLE V. THE CESSATION OF THE BAN

An ecclesiastical prohibition forbidding the celebration of a particular marriage ceased of itself with the passage of the prescribed time for which it was imposed,[109] or with the cessation of the cause for which it was imposed, for instance, with the removal of all doubt and suspicion regarding the possible existence of a diriment impediment through a sentence that proclaimed the freedom of the parties concerned.[110]

The prohibition could also cease through its legitimate revocation by the ecclesiastical prelate who imposed it, or by his superior.[111]

Moreover, when the prohibition was in the form of a precept, it was governed, in general at least,[112] by the norms that were applicable to precepts. The prohibition primarily affected the person because of its intimate association and connection with him, and thus remained applicable even if the person in question went to another diocese and there wished to contract the marriage.[113]

---

108. "Si quis vero huiusmodi clandestina, vel interdicta conjugia inire praesumpserit, in gradu prohibito etiam ignoranter, soboles de tali coniunctione suscepta, prorsus illegitima censeatur, de parentum ignorantia nullum habitura subsidium: cum illi taliter contrahendo non expertes scientiae, vel saltem affectatores ignorantiae videantur." — C. 3, X, *de clandestina desponsatione,* IV, 3.

109. Sanchez, *De Matrimonio,* Lib. VII, Disp. XVII, n. 1.

110. C. 3, X, *de iis qui contrahunt matrimonium contra interdictum ecclesiae,* IV, 16.

111. Wernz, *Ius Matrimoniale,* n. 604.

112. "As a law exists for the common good, so a precept exists for the good of individuals. Consequently, unless limiting clauses are attached to it, a precept follows a private person wherever he may go, as 'the shadow follows the body,' 'it clings to his very bones.' Precepts are binding everywhere; that is, they are extraterritorial, while laws, on the contrary, are presumed to be territorial." — Cicognani, *Canon Law* (second revised edition, Westminster, Maryland: The Newman Bookshop, 1946), p. 635.

113. Wernz, *Ius Matrimoniale,* n. 604, nota 22.

However, that which was generally true concerning the cessation of a precept at the death of the one who imposed it could not be accepted as indiscriminately applicable to a matrimonial prohibition, since the reasons for the imposition of the prohibition, for instance, the scandal that was to be avoided, the doubt alleged concerning the existence of an impediment, etc., existed as factors that were completely independent of the death of the one who imposed the precept. Moreover, such prohibitions seemed to be under the protection and the approbation of the general law. In view, then, of the public good and of the continued sanction of the general law, these matrimonial prohibitions seemed not to lose their binding force at the death of the one who imposed them.[114]

---

114. *Loc. cit.*

PART TWO

CANONICAL COMMENTARY

CHAPTER IV

LEGISLATION OF CANON 1039

The Church's present law which limits the power of local ordinaries in the establishment of matrimonial impediments for their subjects to a mere temporary prohibition in particular cases is the product of a rather extensive historical evolution. From the exclusive viewpoint of the divine law, whether positive or natural, it seems to be within the power of the local bishop to establish diriment impediments for his own diocese, just as it is within the power of the Supreme Pontiff to establish diriment impediments for the Church at large.[1]

In the early days of the Church, local bishops were actually granted the faculty by law of establishing diriment impediments.[2] Subsequently this faculty was revoked, and a local bishop was unable to establish a diriment impediment, even in his own diocese.[3] But it was still within his competence to prohibit a particular marriage in his own diocese.[4] And this prohibition was in reality more than a mere precept; it was a true impediment to marriage; not diriment, but rather impedient.[5]

ARTICLE I. GENERAL CONCEPTS

The present law states that local ordinaries may forbid marriage in particular cases, but only temporarily, for a just cause, and as long as such cause continues to exist, to all persons actually staying within their territory, and to their subjects even outside their territory. Only the Apostolic See has the power to add an invalidating clause to the prohibition.[6]

1. Sanchez, *De Matrimonio,* Lib. VII, Disp. VI, n. 6.
2. Pontius, *De Sacramento Matrimonii Tractatus,* Lib. VI, Cap. VII, p. 227, n. 2.
3. Prosperus Fagnanus, *Commentaria,* Lib. IV, tit. *de matrimonio contracto contra interdictum ecclesiae,* p. 76, n. 10.
4. Schmalzgrueber, *Ius Ecclesiasticum Universum,* Lib. IV, tit. 16, n. 1.
5. Cf. Chapter I, note 4.
6. Canon 1039.

Thus, the Code grants to all *local ordinaries* the power to impose a matrimonial ban in particular cases.[7] The local ordinaries and their successors are conceded this power over all who are actually staying within the limits of their territory, whether they are former inhabitants or newcomers, travelers, or vagrants. Whether or not these persons are the proper subjects of the local ordinary is of no practical import as long as they are actually staying within the limits of his territory.

But if they are not his own proper subjects, actual residence in his territory is required for the validity of the matrimonial ban. It is a necessary condition without which the prohibition would be null and void even though there was present a just cause of itself sufficient to warrant the imposition of a matrimonial ban.[8]

On the other hand, those who are proper subjects of the local ordinary by reason either of domicile or of quasi-domicile[9] are bound to observe the ban whether within or beyond the boundaries of his territory. For precepts obligate the individuals upon whom they are imposed wherever they may be.[10]

For the valid exercise of this power by the local ordinary, *three conditions* must be verified:

1. The marriage on which the ban is imposed must be a *particular* one; that is, for this or that determinate person. It cannot be a general precept, or indeterminate in its mode of imposition. The imposition of a ban by the local ordinary is not even binding for the

---

7. The term *local ordinaries* includes residential bishops, vicars general, vicars and prefects apostolic, and those who succeed the aforementioned in office by prescription of the law. The law indicates as their successors the cathedral chapter if such exists, otherwise the diocesan board of consultors, the administrator, the provicar apostolic, and the proprefect apostolic. Cf. canons 198; 391, §1; 427; 432, §1; 309, §1, §2.

8. Cappello, *Tractatus Canonico-Moralis de Sacramentis,* Vol. V, *De Matrimonio* (ed. quinta, Romae: Marietti, 1947), n. 62 (hereafter cited *De Matrimonio*).

9. Canon 94, §1.

10. Canon 24.

lawfulness of assistance at the marriage if it is general and has not been imposed for this or that marriage in particular.[11]

2. There must be present a *just cause.* In other words, the cause must be grave either in itself or in its circumstances. Thus, if the cause is certainly unjust or false, the prohibition has no obligating force intrinsically, although it may impose an accidental obligation in order that scandal may be avoided. On the other hand, if the cause itself is certain and there is doubt only concerning its gravity, then the prohibition has true binding force, for in cases of doubt, the presumption favors the superior.[12]

Once the just cause has ceased to exist, the prohibition is not to be imposed; and if it has already been imposed, it is to be revoked.[13] Indeed, the prohibition ceases to exist intrinsically by force of law as soon as the proportionate cause has ceased to exist.[14]

Moreover, inasmuch as the local ordinary lacks true legislative power in this matter, he is unable to impose a prohibition which is completely new and unheard of in law, i. e., one which is wholly *praeter ius,* or beyond the scope of the present law. Rather, it is necessary that the just or grave cause be in some way based on the general law itself, and in this sense be taken from the current law, or *secundum ius.*[15]

Some of the just and grave causes which occur rather frequently are: (a) the reasonable dissent of the parents to the marriage of their child who is yet a minor; (b) the prudent suspicion of a hidden impediment, whether diriment or impedient; (c) a truly probable fear

---

11. Sylvius Romani, *Institutiones Iuris Canonici,* Vol. II, *Ius Administrativum de Sacrementis,* Pars Altera, *De Matrimonio* (Romae: Editrice "Iustitia," 1945), n. 724.

12. Cerato, *Matrimonium a Codice I. C. integre Desumptum* (4. ed., Patavii: Typis Seminarii Patavini, 1927), p. 50 (hereafter cited *Matrimonium*).

13. Coronata, *Institutiones Iuris Canonici ad Usum Utriusque Cleri et Scholarum, De Sacramentis Tractatus Canonicus,* Vol. III, *De Matrimonio* (Romae: Marietti, 1946), n. 245 (hereafter cited *De Matrimonio*).

14. "... eaque perdurante." — Canon 1039, §1; Cappello, *loc. cit.*

15. Payen, *De Matrimonio in Missionibus ac Potissimum in Sinis Tractatus Practicus,* Vol. I (altera editio, Zi-ka-wei: in Typographia T'ou-sè-wè, 1935), n. 588 (hereafter cited *De Matrimonio*).

that the marriage will be the occasion of calamities of a serious nature, such as grave scandal, uncommon enmities, or violent strife; (d) an intention which is not indeed invalidating but nevertheless connotes an abuse of marriage and consequently proves sinful; (e) the presence of a social disease unknown to the other party.

3. In addition, the prohibition must be merely *temporary*. The local ordinary does not have the power to impose a matrimonial ban either perpetually or for an indefinite period of time, for the prohibition is of a medicinal nature, rather than vindictive. Therefore, even though it is foreseen that the cause will always exist, the prohibition cannot be imposed perpetually.[16]

But the local ordinary may impose the ban for that period of time which he feels is necessary because of the nature of the cause in each particular case. If the adequate and certain cause ceases to exist before this period of time has expired, then the prohibition of the local ordinary is revoked by provision of the Code.[17]

Since only the Holy See has the power to add an invalidating clause to a matrimonial ban, a marriage contracted in violation of the prohibition of the local ordinary renders the subsequent marriage illicit but does not destroy its validity. Nevertheless, as the prohibition is imposed only for a just and reasonable cause, it establishes a grave obligation in conscience on the part of those affected by the prohibition.[18] Thus, all who violate the prohibition sin gravely even though they believe that there is no justification for its imposition in their case.[19]

ARTICLE II. PARTICULAR ASPECTS

SECTION 1. *The Ban Is a Precept*

An examination of the general concepts of canon 1039 discloses the fact that the imposition of a matrimonial ban by the local ordinary

16. Cerato, *loc. cit.*

17. Canon 1039, §1; Payen, *op. cit.*, I, n. 589.

18. Cappello, *loc. cit.*

19. Gougnard, *Tractatus de Matrimonio* (editio septima, Mechliniae: H. Dessain, 1931), p. 335 (hereafter cited *De Matrimonio*).

is a species of personal precept, for he is able to impose such a prohibition only temporarily.[20]

In addition, the Code explicitly denies to all except the Holy See the power to prohibit marriage by an enactment of law or through the establishment of an impediment in the strict sense of the term: "The same Supreme Authority has the exclusive right to establish for baptized persons impedient or diriment impediments either by way of general or particular law."[21] Thus, the local ordinaries are unable to enact even synodal laws imposing such prohibitions, for this would be equivalent to the establishment of an impedient impediment by particular law. This is expressly forbidden by the aforesaid canon.[22]

Moreover, inasmuch as canon 1039 involves a restriction of the free exercise of the rights of individuals, it must be interpreted strictly.[23] Such a strict interpretation precludes the possibility of the local ordinary's imposing a matrimonial ban in the form of a law, and limits his power to the prohibition of marriage in individual instances only.[24] It is for this reason that Cerato objects to the use of the term "impediment" in conjunction with this power of the local ordinary to prohibit marriage. It is no longer either appropriate or accurate when used to describe this prerogative.[25]

Under the prescriptions of the Code, the power of the local ordinary in imposing this matrimonial ban is equivalent to the imposition of a personal precept, in particular cases, for a just cause. This precept is temporary, rendering all marriages contracted in violation of it illicit, but never directly invalid.[26]

The purpose of the imposition of this matrimonial ban is the obviation of scandal, the prevention of delicts, and the maintenance of the serenity of the social order in general. It is evident, therefore, that it is imposed for the external forum, and is intended both for the

20. Cerato, *loc. cit.*
21. Canon 1038, §2.
22. *Loc. cit.*
23. Canon 19.
24. "... in causa peculiari ..." — Canon 1039.
25. *Op cit.*, p. 51.
26. *Loc. cit.;* Payen, *op. cit.*, I, n. 590.

good of the subject on whom it is imposed and for the good of society in general. As a personal precept, the prohibition of a particular marriage by the local ordinary is governed by the prescriptions of canon 24 as well as by those of canon 1039, §1. Therefore, the local ordinary has power in this regard over those who are not his subjects only as long as they remain in his territory.

A matrimonial ban imposed on a person who is not the proper subject of the local ordinary but who is staying in his territory ceases to have any effect once the person has departed from the territory. On the other hand, if the matrimonial ban is imposed on a person who is a proper subject of the local ordinary, it adheres to the person on whom it is imposed as a personal precept, and accompanies him wherever he goes. It therefore binds the person everywhere unless the local ordinary who imposes it indicates that he intends it to bind only in his territory.[27]

The obligatory force of the precept begins as soon as it is authoritatively intimated to the one upon whom it is imposed. A superior who imposes such a precept without any solemnity of form is considered to accommodate himself to the common practice whereby the binding force of a particular precept is limited to the duration of his period of jurisdiction. It is within his power, however, to extend the binding force of the precept beyond his period of jurisdiction by making use of the solemnity prescribed in canon 24.[28]

---

27. It seems within the power of the local ordinary to limit the binding force of his precept to a certain definite territory if he so desires. Thus, Coronata observes: "Quaestio fit utrum praeceptum de quo in can. 24 ita necessario sequatur personam cui datum est ut superior praeceptum territoriale seu non obligans extra suum territorium dare non possit. Cum vis obligandi quae adnexa est praecepto et ex praecepto directe oritur, ultimo a voluntate superioris praecipientis oriatur, si hic non intendit subditum obligare suo praecepto nisi intra suum territorium, certe, ut videtur, obligatio ultra territorium non extenditur, licet Codex dicat *ubique urgent;* illa enim dictio valere dicenda est pro casibus in quibus superior praecipiens aliud non statuat in ipso praecepto dando." —*Institutiones Iuris Canonici ad Usum Utriusque Cleri et Scholarum* (ed. altera, 5 vols., Taurini: Marietti, 1939-1947), I, n. 33 (hereafter cited *Institutiones*).

28. Wernz-Vidal, *Ius Canonicum ad Codicis Normam Exactum,* Tomus I, *Normae Generales* (Romae: Apud Aedes Universitatis Gregorianae, 1938), n. 200 (hereafter cited *Ius Canonicum*).

This canon states that if a precept is not imposed with a certain solemnity — that is, through a legal document or in the presence of two witnesses — it cannot be enforced judicially, and it ceases to exist with the cessation of the authority of the superior who imposed it. On the other hand, if it is imposed with the solemnity described in this canon, it can be enforced judicially and has binding force independently of the cessation of the authority of the one who imposed it.

The term *legal document* is not specifically defined by the Code as it applies to canon 24. Woywod (1880-1941) was of the opinion that if a letter has the ordinary formalities required in all documents — place, date, signature — and it is plain from the wording of the letter that the local ordinary means to use his authority to impose a precept, such a letter can be called a *legal document* in the sense of canon 24.[29] Coronata also maintains that a private letter of the local ordinary seems to fulfill the requirements in regard to solemnity of form in the imposition of the matrimonial ban as long as a copy is retained in the archives together with the receipt attesting to the fact and date of the delivery of the letter by registered mail to the party in question.[30]

However, Van Hove points out that a legal document needs to be one which proves the facts it asserts.[31] According to the Code, such a document is a public document.[32] Moreover, according to the Code, the acts of ordinaries are equivalent to public documents only when they are issued in the exercise of their office and in authentic form.[33] Consequently, the legal document mentioned in canon 24 must be one which is issued in authentic form. Furthermore, according to Roberti, the acts of ordinaries issued in the exercise of their office are for the

---

29. *A Practical Commentary on the Code of Canon Law* (second ed., 2 vols., New York: Wagner, 1926), I, 16.

30. Coronata, *Institutiones Iuris Canonici,* Vol. IV, *De Delictis et Poenis* (editio altera emendata et aucta, Taurini: Marietti, 1945), n. 1711.

31. *Commentarium Lovaniense in Codicem Iuris Canonici,* Vol. II, *De Legibus Ecclesiasticis* (Mechliniae-Romae: H. Dessain, 1930), n. 363.

32. Canon 1816.

33. Canon 1813, §1; Instruction of the Sacred Congregation of the Sacraments, *Provida,* 15 August, 1936, art. 156, §1; *Acta Apostolicae Sedis, Commentarium Officiale,* XXVIII (1936), 344.

most part signed by the ordinary and a notary, and stamped with the diocesan seal.[34]

Therefore, from the viewpoint of legal procedure, it seems more satisfactory to employ the services of the chancellor in drawing up a legal document, and to affix the diocesan seal thereto.[35]

Moreover, a matrimonial ban which has been imposed through a legal document can be fortified by means of specific penalties to be incurred in the event that the prohibition is violated; for generally those who have the power to make laws or impose precepts are able to attach penalties to them.[36] The vicar general constitutes an exception to this general rule. He has need of a special mandate in order that he may impose penalties.[37] Without this special mandate the vicar general cannot validly attach penalties to a matrimonial ban.[38]

This prohibition is an extrajudicial precept in form, and is ordinarily to be imposed according to the norms of canons 24 and 2225. As such, it may be fortified with the penalties mentioned in canon 1933, §4.[39]

The threatened penalties, like the ban itself, are also governed by the prescriptions of canon 24. Therefore, they can be incurred by those who are not proper subjects of the local ordinary only while they remain subject to him by reason of their presence in his territory. The penalties will not be incurred by such non-subjects once they have left the territory of the local ordinary, for the matrimonial ban itself no longer binds in such circumstances. On the other hand, those who are proper subjects of the local ordinary are subject to the threatened penalties once they have violated the matrimonial ban, wherever they may be. For as they are bound by the matrimonial prohibition everywhere, so also are they subject to the threatened penalties wherever they may be.

---

34. Roberti, *De Processibus,* Vol. II (Romae, 1926), n. 367.

35. Coronata, *loc. cit.*

36. Canon 2220, §1.

37. Canon 2220, §2.

38. Coronata, *Institutiones,* IV, n. 1693; Cappello, *Tractatus Canonico-Moralis de Censuris iuxta Codicem Iuris Canonici* (ed. altera, Taurini: Marietti, 1925), n. 12 (hereafter cited *De Censuris*).

39. Coronata, *ibid.,* n. 1711.

Moreover, even in the case of one not properly subject to the local ordinary, once such a penalty has been declared or inflicted, unless there is express provision to the contrary, it binds him wherever he may be.[40]

If a penalty, either *latae* or *ferendae sententiae,* has been imposed in conjunction with a matrimonial ban, once the ban has been violated the penalty should ordinarily be declared or inflicted in writing or before two witnesses, and the reasons for the penalty should be indicated.[41] A penalty thus declared or inflicted binds the person concerned wherever he may be.[42]

SECTION 2. *Delegation of Power Contained in Canon 1039*

The Code gives to ordinaries of places the power to impose, for a just cause, a ban on particular marriages of their own subjects or of others actually staying in their territory. This power is given by the general law itself, and is attached to an ecclesiastical office, the office of local ordinary.

An ecclesiastical office in the strict sense is a permanent position created either by the divine or the ecclesiastical law, conferred according to the rules of the sacred canons, and entailing some participation in ecclesiastical power, whether of orders or of jurisdiction.[43] The position occupied by the local ordinary adequately fulfills these specifications, and is therefore an ecclesiastical office in the strict sense of the term.

Since the power to prohibit particular marriages as specified in canon 1039 is attached to the office of local ordinary by law, it is a species of ordinary jurisdiction. For ordinary jurisdiction is nothing else than that which is attached to an office by law.[44]

---

40. Canon 2226, §4.

41. Canon 2225.

42. Cocchi, *Commentarium in Codicem Iuris Canonici ad Usum Scholarum* (8 vols., Vol. I, ed. V recognita, Taurini: Marietti, 1938), Lib. I, *Normae Generales,* n. 129.

43. Canon 145, §1.

44. Canon 197, §1.

Unless the contrary is expressly provided for by law, whoever enjoys ordinary jurisdiction, whether it is proper or vicarious, may delegate it to another; and he may bestow it on another in any measure or extent that he chooses.[45] He may commit, therefore, any part of his power, either for a single act or for a species of acts; or he may delegate his entire power. However, this latter may be done only with a certain qualification, for an ordinary magistrate may not yield to another the plenitude of his power without restriction of time, or without reservation of anything to himself. For this act would be equivalent to abdication and to the designation of another ordinary, which cannot be done without the permission of the Supreme Superior.[46]

The power which the local ordinary possesses in virtue of canon 1039 is ordinary power; but it is not the plenitude of his ordinary power. It is not the complete and total power which he possesses from the law by reason of his office. It is merely the power which he possesses from the law for a certain definite species of act, that is, the temporary prohibition, for a just cause, of particular marriages of his subjects or of others actually staying in his territory. Since the law makes no express provision to the contrary, he may delegate this power to another, for instance, to the chancellor if he so desires. And he may delegate the entire power which he possesses for this species of act.

However, the vicar general does not possess all the power enjoyed by the other local ordinaries in imposing this ban, for he is unable, without a special mandate, to annex penalties to the violation of his prohibition.[47] Consequently, the power delegated by him in connection

---

45. Canon 199, §1.

46. This is the general opinion of the authors. — Coronata, *Institutiones,* I, n. 288; Cappello, *Summa Iuris Canonici in Usum Scholarum,* Vol. I (editio quarta accurate recognita, Romae: Apud Aedes Universitatis Gregorianae, 1945), n. 260 (hereafter cited *Summa*); Wernz-Vidal, *Ius Canonicum,* Vol. II (ed. 3., Romae: Apud Aedes Universitatis Gregorianae, 1943), n. 369; Chelodi, *Ius Canonicum de Personis* (ed. 3., Trento: Libreria Moderna Editrice, 1942), n. 127, p. 208, in nota 1.

47. Canon 2220, §2.

with canon 1039 is not so extensive as the power delegated by other local ordinaries.

There are several ways in which the power thus delegated by the local ordinary can be extinguished. Generally, the power of the delegate does not expire along with the cessation of the power of the active subject or delegator. The cessation primarily depends upon the mandate itself.[48] The delegation ends with the death of the delegator only if the mandate so provides.[49]

The delegation ceases upon the fulfillment of the task for which the mandate was issued, if it was issued for a certain task only. When the delegate has brought his mandate to a valid execution, his power has run its course. If the mandate is conceded for a definite period of time, the delegation ends when that period has ceased to be. The duration of the time, in such a case, is to be computed according to canons 32-34. A mandate granted *ad beneplacitum nostrum* expires with the death of the delegator; this is not the case, however, if it is granted *ad beneplacitum Sedis* or *ad beneplacitum Ordinarii.* The form, *ad beneplacitum Episcopi,* can be regarded as referring to the dignity, so that it does not end with the death of the incumbent of the office. If it is given *donec revocavero,* it does not cease with the death of the delegator, but requires an explicit act of revocation.[50] Delegation granted for a certain number of cases ends when the delegate has validly acted the specified number of times. And, from the very nature of delegation, the mandate perishes when the final cause for which it was granted totally ceases.

The delegation can also cease by revocation on the part of the delegator; but the Code requires that the revocation be made known directly to the delegate. Hence, the recall does not take effect until the delegate is notified of the same.[51] In the case of renunciation on the part of the delegate, for the delegation to expire it is not sufficient

48. Canon 207, §1.

49. Canon 61.

50. Kearney, *The Principles of Delegation,* The Catholic University of America Canon Law Studies, n. 55 (Washington, D.C.: The Catholic University of America, 1929), p. 114.

51. Canon 207, §1.

that the delegate renounce his power; the renunciation must be made known directly to the delegator, and it must be accepted by him. If the delegator refuses to accept, the delegation still endures.[52]

The Code does not state that the delegation ends with the death of the delegate. Nevertheless, in the case of power to impose a matrimonial ban which is delegated by the local ordinary, it seems that it does end with the death of the delegate unless the delegation is *real,* that is, unless the power is committed to the person in view of his office or dignity.[53]

SECTION 3. *The Power of the Vicar General in Relation to Canon 1039*

Among those included in the category of local ordinaries is the vicar general.[54] As one of this group, it is within his power to impose a matrimonial ban temporarily and for a just cause, in particular instances, on his subjects or on those actually staying within the limits of his territory.[55]

The position held by the vicar general is an ecclesiastical office, and this power to impose a matrimonial ban is attached to the office by law.[56] Thus, this power of the vicar general to prohibit particular marriages is a species of ordinary jurisdiction. As such it may be delegated to another, unless the contrary is stated in the law.[57] And as the contrary is not stated in the law, the vicar general may delegate to another his power to impose a matrimonial ban temporarily and in particular instances, for a just cause, on marriages of his subjects or of those actually staying within the limits of his territory.

However, his powers are not so extensive in regard to the matrimonial ban as are those of the local bishop. For the local bishop is empowered to annex penalties to the violation of his prohibition. The vicar general is unable to do this without a special mandate.[58]

52. *Loc. cit.*
53. Cf. Kearney, *op. cit.,* p. 115.
54. Canon 198, §1.
55. Canon 1039, §1.
56. Canons 368, §1; 145, §1.
57. Canons 197, §1; 199, §1.
58. Canon 2220, §2.

Blat states very explicitly that in virtue of the limitation expressed in canon 2220, §2, the vicar general does not have the power to annex penalties, whether medicinal or vindictive, and that he cannot punish with a penalty any transgression of the law.[59]

Chelodi interprets the wording of this canon in the sense that the vicar general does not have the power to enact (*statuendi*) penalties.[60] Coronata, however, interprets the wording of the canon, not in this limited sense, but in the wider sense of both enacting and inflicting penalties, and thus denies to the vicar general the power either to enact a penal law or to subject a delinquent to a penalty determined in the law.[61]

Salucci, holding a similar opinion, states that the vicar general is unable to enact a penalty, and can apply a penalty only when delegated, and even then only for an individual case.[62] Cappello and Chelodi-Ciprotti likewise state that the vicar general cannot even apply a penalty unless he is at the same time the *officialis,* or unless he has been delegated to do so.[63]

Briefly, then, the vicar general is unable to annex a penalty to a matrimonial ban, and cannot punish the violation of his prohibition of a particular marriage with the infliction of a penalty without first having received a special mandate. Since he is unable to do this himself, it is apparent that without this special mandate he is unable

---

59. *Commentarium Textus Codicis Iuris Canonici,* Liber V, *De Delictis et Poenis* (Romae, 1924), n. 38.

60. *Ius Poenale et Ordo Procedendi in Iudiciis Criminalibus iuxta Codicem Iuris Canonici* (Tridenti: Libr. Edit. Tridentum, 1925), n. 24, nota 2.

61. "... non potest, ne valide quidem, poenas legi aut praecepto a se dato adnectere; nec sententia condemnatoria reum poenae a iure latae subiicere." — *Institutiones,* IV, n. 1693.

62. *Il Diritto Penale Secondo il Codice di Diritto Canonico* (2 vols. in 1, Subiaco: Tipografia dei Monasteri, 1926-1930), p. 99, nota 1.

63. Cappello, *De Censuris,* n. 14; Chelodi-Ciprotti, *Ius Canonicum de Delictis et Poenis et de Iudiciis Criminalibus* (ed. 5., Trento: Libreria Moderna Editrice, 1943), n. 25 (hereafter cited *De Delictis et Poenis*).

to delegate to another the power to annex penalties to a matrimonial ban or to inflict penalties for the violation of the ban.

Similarly, if the power to annex penalties to a matrimonial ban or to inflict penalties for its violation is delegated to him for an individual case only, the vicar general is unable to subdelegate this power to another, unless this faculty has been expressly conceded to him in the mandate.[64] However, if the mandate is given to him for such cases in general, and not for an individual case only, it is then within his competency to delegate this power to others.[65]

Moreover, if one who is delegated by the vicar general when acting without a special mandate to impose a matrimonial prohibition exceeds his authority and attempts to annex a penalty to the prohibition, the penalty is null and void. For one acting with delegated power acts invalidly when he exceeds the limits of his mandate,[66] and a delegate who attempts to annex a penalty to the prohibition without having been delegated to do so is exceeding the limits of his mandate. This must be interpreted in the sense that the delegate acts invalidly only insofar as he *exceeds* his mandate, according to the principle: *Utile non debet per inutile vitiari.*[67]

Similarly, one who has been delegated by the vicar general when acting without a special mandate cannot inflict a penalty on a delinquent who has violated a valid matrimonial prohibition. For without a special mandate, the power to inflict such a penalty cannot be delegated by the vicar general, since under such circumstances he does not even possess the power to inflict such a penalty himself.[68]

Although it is beyond the power of the vicar general to annex penalties to his matrimonial ban or to inflict penalties for its violation, this power can be granted him by means of a special mandate of the local bishop.[69]

---

64. Canon 199, §4.
65. *Ibid.*, §1, §3.
66. Canon 203, §1.
67. Reg. 37, R. J., in VI°.
68. Coronata, *Institutiones,* IV, n. 1693.
69. Canon 2220, §2.

It is not necessary that a written document be used either for the validity or for the lawfulness of the grant of the mandate.[70] For when such is needed for validity, it is expressly indicated by the Code.[71]

However, in practice, the special mandate should be granted in writing in order to preclude all doubts and questions concerning its actual existence. The mandate may be given in a general form for all cases, or for a particular case only, according to the intention of the local bishop who grants it.

Whether the vicar general who acts in virtue of a special mandate acts with ordinary or delegated power is disputed among the authors. Since the time of Boniface VIII (1294-1303), it has been generally recognized that the power enjoyed by the vicar general in virtue of his office is ordinary power. The glossator described the *officialis* or *vicarius* of the bishop, who was the forerunner of the vicar general, as having ordinary power.[72] And Sanchez explicitly attributed this ordinary jurisdiction to the vicar general of the bishop.[73]

Barbosa pointed out that although the vicar general was appointed by the bishop, he received his jurisdiction from the law,[74] and therefore must have ordinary jurisdiction.[75]

---

70. Cappello, *Summa,* I, n. 400.

71. *Loc. cit.*

72. "Qui interdum *missus dominicus* appellatur. Officialis iste ordinariam habet iurisdictionem . . . sequitur quod ex iurisdictione ordinaria hoc facit, non ex delegata . . . negari non possit eos iurisdictionem habere ordinariam." — *Glossa Ordinaria,* ad c. 2, *de officio vicarii,* I, 13, in VI°.

73. *De Matrimonio,* Lib. III, Disp. XXIX, n. 13.

74. ". . . respondetur negando Vicarium iurisdictionem ab episcopo accipere. Nam licet Episcopus Vicarium constituat, et ob eius nominationem officium exerceat, protinus tamen quod ab Episcopo constituitur, lex illi iurisdictionem tribuit, ideo non recte dicitur ab ipso episcopo iurisdictionem accipere, sed a iure potius, ministerio facto, et nominatione Episcopi interveniente." — Barbosa, *Pastoralis Solicitudinis sive De Officio et Potestate Episcopi,* Pars III (Lugduni, 1556), alleg. 54, nn. 44 and 45 (hereafter cited *De Officio et Potestate Episcopi*).

75. " . . . Ex quibus omnibus colligitur generalem Episcopi Vicarium ordinaria sibi a lege concessa non delegata iurisdictione potiri." — *Loc. cit.*

Reiffenstuel reiterated the same principle: jurisdiction received from the law by reason of an office is ordinary jurisdiction.[76] And he was most explicit in his emphasis of the fact that the vicar general received his jurisdiction from the law itself rather than from the bishop.[77]

Since the promulgation of the Code of Canon Law, there has been no dispute regarding the nature of the power held by a vicar general in his office. It is a power which is derived from an office established in law, but which is exercised in another's name.[78] It is the function of the vicar general to be of aid to the bishop; and his acts are to be considered as the acts of the bishop himself.[79]

The vicar general, then, is juridically one with the bishop. And the power by which he acts is the same power by which the bishop acts. For insofar as the vicar general acts by reason of his office but in the name of the bishop, he acts with vicarious ordinary power. And vicarious ordinary power is a species of ordinary power.[80]

However, there still remains the question of the nature of the power of the vicar general when he acts by reason of a special mandate. Canonists are divided in their views as to whether the vicar general acts with ordinary power when this special mandate is given, or

---

76. "... quia iurisdictio, quae a lege, seu canone, ratione officii, seu dignitatis cuipiam conceditur est ordinaria." — *Ius Canonicum Universum* (5 vols. in 7, Parisiis, 1864-1870), Vol. I, tit. *de officio vicarii,* Lib. I, tit. 28, n. 92.

77. "... vicarius generalis episcopi habet iurisdictionem a canone et ratione sui officii sibi concessam.... Nec obstat quod episcopus instituit, seu constituit sibi vicarium generalem. Nam eo ipso, quod is constitutus fuit ab episcopo, ius tribuit ipsi iurisdictionem, et quidem immediate.... Etsi enim episcopus mediet quasi nominans, et instituens, non tamen mediat quasi dans iurisdictionem." — *Loc. cit.*

78. "Quoties rectum dioecesis regimen id exigat, constituendus est ab episcopo Vicarius Generalis, qui ipsum potestate ordinaria in toto territorio adiuvet." — Canon 366, §1.

79. "Vicarius generalis est sacerdos legitime deputatus ad exercendum in toto territorio iurisdictionem episcopalem vice episcopi, ita ut actus eius ab episcopo gesti censeantur." — Vermeersch-Creusen, *Epitome Iuris Canonici* (3 vols., ed. sexta, Mechliniae-Romae: H. Dessain, 1937-1946), I, n. 476 (hereafter cited *Epitome*).

80. Canon 197, §2.

whether the mandate is rather to be interpreted as an indication of delegation.

Roelker is of the opinion that the solution of this controversy depends not strictly on the nature of the power of the vicar general, but rather on the extent of the power conceded in canon 368, §1.[81] He says:

> Should the restriction demonstrated by the necessity of a special mandate so effectively limit the extent of the vicar general's office that the power of his office is essentially less than universal, it must be maintained that a special mandate indicates delegation. Therefore, an act performed with this special mandate is the result of delegated power. Should, however, the restriction in canon 368, §1, be considered not as subtraction but rather as a suspension of power fundamentally universal, a removal of the restriction would merely remove a hindrance to operate. In this way, a special mandate would not indicate delegation but rather an authorization to act. Such an act, then, would be performed by reason of the power of the vicar general's office and should be considered as ordinary power.[82]

Roelker feels, therefore, that the nature of the mandate does not touch the real point at issue. It is his opinion that if the vicar general does not possess fundamentally complete jurisdiction, a mandate given to him to act jurisdictionally must contain delegated power; but if the vicar general does possess fundamentally complete jurisdiction, the mandate only releases power hitherto restricted. Roelker then asserts the concept of fundamentally complete jurisdiction as the correct interpretation of canon 368, §1,[83] and so aligns himself with

---

81. "Vicario Generali, vi officii, ea competit in universa dioecesi iurisdictio in spiritualibus ac temporalibus, quae ad episcopum iure ordinario pertinet, exceptis iis quae Episcopus sibi reservaverit, vel quae ex iure requirant speciale Episcopi mandatum."

82. "The Vicar General and the Special Mandate," *The Jurist* (Washington, D. C., 1941-), II (1942), 349.

83. *Ibid.*, pp. 358, 359.

those canonists who maintain that the vicar general acts with ordinary power even when he needs and obtains a special mandate.[84]

Others are of the opinion that the vicar general uses delegated power in these cases.[85] In presenting this opinion, Kearney says:[86]

> . . . by a special mandate [the bishop] confers powers which the common law has effectively detached from the office of Vicar. In this case the Vicar, receiving the power, accepts something that is not attached by law to his office. It is, therefore, delegation.

In the consideration of this question, it should be noted that the exclusion of certain functions from the competence of the vicar general is no innovation. Such was the case as early as the time of Boniface VIII.[87] Barbosa explained that by virtue of his general power the vicar general could not perform those functions which required a special mandate.[88] Reiffenstuel stated that the vicar general could ordinarily do all things which were within the power of the bishop,

---

84. Wernz-Vidal, *Ius Canonicum,* Vol. II, *De Personis* (ed. tertia, Romae: Apud Aedes Universitatis Gregorianae, 1943), n. 640; Vermeersch-Creusen, *op. cit.,* I, n. 479; Stutz, *Der Geist des Codex iuris canonici, Kirchenrechtliche Abhandlungen,* 92. und 93. Heft (Stuttgart: Verlag von Ferdinand Enke, 1918), p. 325; Coronata, *Institutiones,* I, n. 421.

85. Chelodi, *Ius de Personis iuxta Codicem Iuris Canonici* (Tridenti: Libr. Edit. Tridentum, 1927), p. 330; Kearney, *op. cit.,* pp. 72-74; Toso, "Summa de Officio et Potestate Vicarii Generalis," *Jus Pontificium* (Romae, 1921-1940), VII (1927), 138-146, n. 12; Bastnagel, "Doubtful Competence of the Vicar General," *The Jurist,* VIII (1948), 213-219; Regatillo, *Institutiones Iuris Canonici* (ed. secunda, 2 vols., Santander: Sal Terrae, 1946), I, 266; Beste, *Introductio in Codicem* (ed. 3., Collegeville, Minn.: St. John's Abbey Press, 1946), p. 276.

86. *Loc. cit.*

87. "Licet in officialem episcopi per commissionem offici, generaliter sibi factam, causarum cognitio transferatur, potestatem tamen inquirendi, corrigendi, aut puniendi aliquorum excessus, seu aliquos a suis beneficiis, officiis, vel administrationibus amovendi, transferri nolumus in eundem, nisi sibi specialiter haec committantur." — C. 2, *de officio vicarii,* I, 13, in VI°.

88. "In generali Vicarii concessione conceduntur ea tantum quae in generali mandato continentur . . . non tamen potest ea . . . quae speciale postulant mandatum." — *De Officio et Potestate Episcopi,* III, alleg. 54, n. 59.

exclusive of those things which were specially excepted by law.[89] Schmalzgrueber also indicated that the general power of the vicar general did not extend to those matters which required a special mandate.[90]

The infliction of penalties was one of the matters which was not included in the general power of the vicar general.[91] Barbosa stated that the vicar general was unable to prosecute criminal causes without a special mandate, and mentioned the imposition of penalties as one of the functions prohibited under this classification.[92] Wernz excluded from the power of the vicar general the authority to remove another from an office or from a benefice.[93]

Reiffenstuel further explained that criminal causes were removed from the competence of the vicar general because they involved capital punishment and the infliction of serious penalties. If the vicar general ignored the law and presided over criminal causes without a special mandate, the trial was null and void due to lack of jurisdiction.[94]

---

89. "Vicarius generalis episcopi per commissionem officii sui sibi generaliter factam, regulariter potest ea omnia, quae ipsi episcopo concessa intelliguntur; nisi fuerint specialiter in iure excepta . . . tacendo ea quae in iure specialiter sunt excepta (de his enim nulla amplius subesse potest dubitatio)." Vol. I, tit. *de officio vicarii,* Lib. I, tit. 28, nn. 76 and 78.

90. *Ius Ecclesiasticum Universum,* Lib. I, tit. 28, n. 21.

91. "Ex generali commissione non potest officialis inquirere, corrigere, deponere, et punire subditorum excessus." — *Glossa Ordinaria,* ad c. 2, *de officio vicarii,* I, 13, in VI°, s. v. *licet.*

92. ". . . nec criminales causas, nisi specialiter commissae fuerunt, expedire poterit, ita ut nec inquirere, corrigere, aut punire subditorum excessus queat." — *De Officio et Potestate Episcopi,* Pars III, alleg. 54, n. 117.

93. "Ex ipsa iuris dispositione vicarius generalis sine mandato speciali nequit . . . inquirere, corrigere, aut punire aliquorum excessus seu aliquos a suis beneficiis, officiis, vel administrationibus amovere." — *Ius Decretalium,* Tom. II, p. 990.

94. "Excipiuntur autem in primis causae criminales, utpote quae inter negotia magis ardua connumerantur; cum in eis tractetur de vita hominis, et de poena graviter infligenda. . . . Ac proinde in generali mandato non veniunt, sed opus est speciali expressione. . . . Atque hoc adeo verum est, ut si vicarius generalis sese causis criminalibus absque speciali mandato intromittat, processus ipso jure sit irritus ob defectum jurisdictionis." — Reiffenstuel, *Ius Canonicum Universum,* Vol. I, tit. *de officio vicarii,* Lib. I, tit. 28, n. 80.

This doctrine was in accordance with a decretal of Boniface VIII, whereby the power of inflicting punishment was not included in the general competence of the vicar general. Consequently, a special commission was required in order that the vicar general have competency over such causes.[95]

Although the vicar general did not have the power to impose penalties without a special mandate, if such a special mandate was given to him, he then imposed the penalties through the use of ordinary power.[96] For the jurisdiction to impose penalties was given as an accessory to the office of vicar general, and therefore had to conform to the nature of his office. Since the vicar general acted in virtue of ordinary power, he also with the use of ordinary power performed those functions which were included in his jurisdiction by means of a special mandate.[97]

---

95. "...Cum Pontifex praemisisset [c. 2, *de officio vicarii,* I, 13, in VI°] quod per commissionem officii generaliter factam officiali episcopi, causarum cognitio in eum transferatur, illico, notanter subiungit: 'Potestatem tamen inquirendi, corrigendi, aut puniendi aliquorum excessus, seu aliquos a suis beneficiis, officiis, vel administrationibus amovendi, transferri nolumus in eumdem: nisi specialiter haec committantur.' Hactenus Pontifex." — *Loc. cit.*

96. "Vicarius generalis episcopi habet jurisdictionem ordinariam non tantum in iis causis, quae ex generali officio vicariatus ipsi competunt, et in generali mandato vicariatus comprehenduntur: sed etiam in iis, quae speciali commissione opus habent, modo, vel in prima commissione generali Vicariatus officio specialiter annectantur, vel tamquam Generali Vicario, seu intuitu officii Vicariatus, postea per speciale mandatum committantur." — Pirhing, *Ius Canonicum in Quinque Libros Decretalium Distributum Nova Methodo Explicatum,* Tomus Primus (Dilingae, 1674), Lib. I, tit. 28, *De Officio Vicarii,* n. 40 (hereafter cited *Ius Canonicum*). Cf. also Sanchez, *De Matrimonio,* Lib. III, Disp. XXIX, n. 8; Reiffenstuel, *ibid.,* n. 94.

97. "Ratio est quia... iurisdictio, quoad actus specialem commissionem exigentes, datur tamquam annexa, et accessoria ad ipsum officium generale vicariatus, et ideo sicut iurisdictio principalis ipsius officii generalis vicariatus est ordinaria: ita, et iurisdictio, quoad actus specialiter commissos, accessorie ipsi annexa transit in ordinariam, quia accessorium sequitur naturam principalis, iuxta *reg. iur.* 42 in VI°." — Pirhing, *loc. cit.;* "... quia tota iurisdictio vicarii generalis erit ordinaria.... Ratio est: quia connexorum idem est iudicium.... Simulque accessorium naturam sequitur principalis.... Atqui in posito casu, iurisdicto quoad causas specialiter commissas est annexa, simulque accessoria ad iurisdictionem ordinariam vicarii generalis." — Reiffenstuel, *Ius Canonicum*

This did not apply to those functions which were committed to him in particular cases and not as a part of his general power. Such functions were, in general, performed in virtue of delegated power only.[98] The only exception was the case in which such power was given to the vicar general in a particular instance by reason of his being a vicar, or by reason of his office. In such a case the vicar general acted by reason of ordinary power.[99]

Therefore, prior to the Code, it was recognized that for delegated jurisdiction it was necessary that a person be acting only by commission of another, and not by reason of any office to which this jurisdiction was connected by law. It was for this reason that the vicar general was not considered to act by delegated power: for he received his jurisdiction from the law by reason of his office, despite the fact that this jurisdiction was capable of extension or restriction by the bishop who constituted him in office.[100] Although he was powerless to impose

---

Universum, Vol. I, tit. *de officio vicarii,* Lib. I, tit. 28, n. 94. Cf. also Sanchez, *De Matrimonio,* Lib. III, Disp. XXIX, n. 8.

---

98. "In iis vero causis specialibus, quae in prima commissione, seu constitutione vicarii ipsi specialiter non committuntur, sed postea seorsim, ac separatim per speciale mandatum delegantur, non tamen intuitu, aut sub nomine vicariatus, iurisdictionem delegatam tantum habet vicarius." — Pirhing, *loc. cit.* "Secus dicendum de illis quae non solum requirunt speciale mandatum, sed insuper seorsim ac singulariter eidem committuntur: quia in istis iurisdictio est delegata . . . nam iurisdictio, quae ad actus separatim et singulariter commissos datur, non potest censeri annexa vel accessoria ad generale officium vicariatus: ideoque recte delegata dici debet." — Reiffenstuel, *ibid.,* n. 95.

99. "Nisi Episcopus talia committat vicario generali ut vicario. Verumtamen hoc ipsum limitant doctores, quando episcopus postea singularem causam, speciali mandato indigentem, committit generali vicario tamquam vicario, seu intuitu officii vicariatus: quia tunc etiam quoad hanc causam censebitur iurisdictio vicarii esse ordinaria." — Reiffenstuel, *ibid.,* n. 96.

100. "Requiritur ergo inter alia ad iurisdictionem delegatam, quod quis vices alterius gerat, non ex ullo proprio officio, cui talis iurisdictio de iure cohaereat, sed ex nuda commissione alterius. Hoc autem non fit in proposito, cum vicario generali competat sua iurisdictio a iure vi proprii officii; haud obstante quod per episcopum, qui ipsum constituit, ea ampliari vel restringi valeat." — Reiffenstuel, *ibid.,* n. 99.

penalties without a special mandate, nevertheless when he acted in virtue of a special mandate which authorized his use of this power — not one that was given for an individual case only — the vicar general imposed penalties by reason of jurisdiction received from the law because of his office. In other words, he exercised ordinary power.

There does not seem to be any substantial change in the concept of ordinary jurisdiction since the promulgation of the Code. Under the law of the Code, ordinary jurisdiction is that which is connected with an office;[101] but only that which is connected with the office in a special way — namely, by law.[102] It is for this reason that powers connected with an office by privilege rather than by law are not ordinary, but delegated.[103]

Furthermore, in order that the jurisdiction be ordinary, it must be connected with the office by law in a more or less permanent manner. The verification of such a power in single instances only is not sufficient to constitute ordinary jurisdiction.[104]

Moreover, the exact scope or extent of this power may depend upon the permission or mandate of some superior, but in such a way that

---

101. "Potestas igitur, ut sit ordinaria debet esse officio adnexa ex iure *antecedenter* ad personas quae exercere debeant potestatem; est nimirum aliquid inhaerens officio tamquam praevium et independens a personis quae officium obtineant; proinde non committitur directe personis sed acquiritur *consequenter* ex officii acquisitione et proinde similiter amittitur ex amissione officii." — Maroto, *Institutiones Iuris Canonici ad Normam Novi Codicis* (2 vols., Vol. I, 3. ed., Romae, 1921), n. 699, 10° (hereafter cited *Institutiones*).

102. "Potestas iurisdictionis ordinaria ea est quae ipso iure adnexa est officio." — Canon 197, §1.

103. "Similiter delegata est potestas quae adnexa quodammodo sit officio, at non ex iure sed ex privilegio stricte sumpto; atque adeo facultates habituales etiam perpetuae, quae concedi solent ordinariis (cf. c. 66) sunt accensendae potestati delegatae non ordinariae." — Maroto, *op. cit.*, I, n. 699, 6°.

104. "Item debet esse *permanenter* officio adiecta, iuxta naturam ipsius officii quod stabiliter constituitur (c. 145); ergo numquam habenda est ut ordinaria potestas illa singularis facultas quae in casu particulari tribuatur ad aliquid agendum, exsequendum, etc., licet censeatur concessa non personae sed officio." — Maroto, *ibid.*, 11°.

the power does not originate from the mandate of the superior; rather, it comes from the law itself by reason of the office which the person holds, and depends upon the mandate of the superior for its extent only.[105] In other words, under the Code today, ordinary jurisdiction is in certain cases capable of restriction or extension according to the will of the superior. If the superior restricts the ordinary power of his inferiors, such inferiors *per se* have no power to act in the restricted cases at all. If the superior does not restrict their powers, they act in such circumstances by virtue of ordinary power.[106] Thus, for instance, a superior may restrict the ordinary power of his inferiors by reserving to himself the absolution in the external forum of certain censures imposed by him either by way of law or of precept.[107]

In the interpretation of the law of the Code as it exists today, the canons which restate the earlier law in its entirety must be interpreted in accordance with the earlier law,[108] and hence the interpretations already given by approved authors are to be followed in the interpretation of these laws of the Code. By "the earlier law" the Code means all previous legislation, and it decrees that those canons which restate the earlier legislation without change must be interpreted upon the authority of the earlier law. The earlier law has juridical force only inasmuch as it is embodied in the Code, but it is the

---

105. "Adiectio potestatis quandoque praerequirit specialem veniam seu mandatum alicuius superioris; quo supposito, potestas censetur competere non vi ipsius mandati vel veniae a superiore datae sed vi iuris et ex officio, ipsaque potestas habenda est ut ordinaria." — Maroto, *ibid.,* 9°.

106. "Potest item ordinaria iurisdictio restringi, officio remanente in individuo vel etiam in specie, subtractione personarum subditarum quibus exemptio a iure aut a superiore concedatur, subtractione loci seu territorii subiecti quod evenire potest concessione exemptionis; dismembratione aut divisione officiorum; itemque reservatione a superiore facta casuum aut officiorum ecclesiasticorum." — Coronata, *Institutiones,* I, n. 281; ". . . quoad partem iurisdictio, manente officio, potest limitari vel restringi sive quoad personas, loca, etc., per exemptionem (cf. cc. 615, 464, §2) sive quoad res per reservationem (cf. cc. 893, 1435, 2245)." — Maroto, *op. cit.,* I, n. 703, 5°.

107. Canon 2245, §4.

108. Canon 6, 2°.

interpretive norm of the new law whenever the new and the old coincide.[109]

Furthermore, those canons which restate the earlier law must be explained according to the interpretations given by approved authors, that is, conformably to the former teaching and jurisprudence.[110] Even in the case wherein it is doubtful whether some provision of the canons differs from the earlier law, the earlier law must be followed.[111] Thus, wherever there is a positive doubt, or indeed an opinion of a discrepancy between the present and the earlier law, no departure must be made from the earlier law, nor from the old teaching and jurisprudence.[112]

Moreover, under the present law of the Code, ordinary power of jurisdiction is to be broadly interpreted.[113]

Consequently, since apparently there is no discrepancy, or at most only a doubt as to any discrepancy between the law of the Code and the earlier law in regard to the power used by the vicar general in matters which require a special mandate,[114] and since prior to the Code the vicar general did not have the power to impose penalties without a special mandate, but imposed them by ordinary power if such a mandate was given to him,[115] it seems only logical to conclude that under the present law of the Code the vicar general has no power to impose penalties without a special mandate, but that once he has received the required mandate he acts in virtue of ordinary power unless it is expressly stated in the mandate that he is being delegated

---

109. Neuberger, *Canon 6 or the Relation of the Codex Iuris Canonici to Preceding Legislation,* The Catholic University of America Canon Law Studies, n. 44 (Washington, D. C.: The Catholic University of America, 1927), p. 70.

110. Canon 6, 2°.

111. Canon 6, 4°.

112. Cicognani, *Canon Law,* p. 504.

113. Canon 200, §1.

114. "Cum in hac parte [quali potestate utatur vicarius generalis in negotiis quae mandatum speciale requirunt] nihil differat a iure praecedenti nisi per taxativam enumerationem eorum, quae mandato speciali egent." — Wernz-Vidal, *Ius Canonicum,* II, n. 640.

115. Pirhing, *Ius Canonicum,* Lib. I, tit. 28, n. 40; Sanchez, *De Matrimonio,* Lib. III, Disp. XXIX, n. 8; Reiffenstuel, *Ius Canonicum Universum,* Vol. I, tit. *de officio vicarii,* Lib. I, tit. 28, n. 94.

for a single instance only, in which case he would act in virtue of delegated power.[116]

Even those canonists who would disagree with this conclusion, and who maintain that a vicar general always acts in virtue of delegated power when acting with a special mandate, would agree that without the special mandate the vicar general is unable to impose penalties. In either case, then, whether he acts by ordinary or delegated power when acting with a special mandate, the vicar general is unable to annex or inflict penalties without a special mandate.

In regard to the possible delegation of this power, the preferable opinion seems to be that a vicar general who has a special mandate empowering him to annex and inflict penalties may delegate it to another in any measure or extent that he chooses.[117] However, those who maintain that the vicar general who acts in virtue of a special mandate acts with delegated power would conclude that he could delegate this power in single instances only.[118]

---

116. "Ita vicarius generalis in iis quae episcopi mandatum speciale requirunt, non potest agere sine ipso mandato; postquam vero episcopus illud mandatum praestiterit, tunc vicarius generalis agit ut vicarius et potestate ordinaria, non ut delegatus episcopi." — Maroto, *op. cit.,* I, n. 699, 9°; "Quare sicut episcopus auferens reservationem initio muneris factam, non videtur conferre delegationem, sed ampliare iurisdictionem ordinariam, ita per concessionem mandati specialis, tametsi non initio muneris factam, censerem fieri eamdem ampliationem potestatis ordinariae, nisi *expresse* constituatur *delegatus* ad unum actum mandatum speciale requirentem." — Wernz-Vidal, *loc. cit.;* "restrictione autem relaxata per mandatum speciale, ipse iurisdictione quae ei ex iure ordinario pertinet, vi officii, utitur." — Coronata, *Institutiones,* I, n. 421.

117. Canon 199, §1.

118. Canon 199, §3.

CHAPTER V

CAUSES SUFFICIENT TO WARRANT THE IMPOSITION OF A MATRIMONIAL BAN

In order to warrant the imposition of a matrimonial ban, the cause must be grave both in itself and by reason of the circumstances of the case. Moreover, the nature of the reason for prohibiting the marriage must be in accordance with the general law of the Church, for local ordinaries are incompetent to introduce some new reason for forbidding marriage.[1] It is not necessary, however, that the cause be stated explicitly in the general law in order that the local ordinary may act. It is sufficient that it be in keeping with the fundamental and general principles of law concerning the valid and lawful contract of a particular marriage under such circumstances.[2]

The causes treated herein are not proposed as exhausting the field. They are presented explicitly because of the importance of their subject matter and the frequency with which they occur.

ARTICLE I. THE REASONABLE DISSENT OF THE PARENTS OF MINORS

Authors agree in teaching that reasonable dissent on the part of parents is a just and grave cause for forbidding a particular marriage which involves a child of minor age.[3]

Both the right and the duty of determining the reasonableness or unreasonableness of the parental dissent in regard to the marriage of their children of minor age rests with the pastor, who has the obligation

1. Payen, *De Matrimonio,* I, n. 588.

2. Wernz-Vidal, *Ius Matrimoniale* (ed. 3., Romae: Apud Aedes Universitatis Gregorianae, 1946), n. 55.

3. Cappello, *De Matrimonio;* n. 192; Rossi, *De Matrimonii Celebratione iuxta Codicem Iuris Canonici* (Romae: Fridericus Pustet, 1924), p. 54; De Smet, *Tractatus Theologico-Canonicus de Sponsalibus et Matrimonio* (4. ed., Brugis: Car Beyaert, 1927), n. 487; Vermeersch-Creusen, *Epitome,* II, n. 299; Payen, *loc. cit.;* Cerato, *Matrimonium,* p. 51; Claeys Bouuaert-Simenon, *Manuale Iuris Canonici ad usum Seminariorum,* Vol. II (Gandae et Leodii: Apud Auctores in Seminariis Gandanensi et Leodiensi, 1931), n. 246; Gougnard, *De Matrimonio,* p. 30; Blat, *Commentarium Textus Codicis Iuris Canonici,* Vol. III (2. ed., Romae, 1924), n. 431.

to conduct the prenuptial investigation and enjoys the right to assist at the marriage.[4] If the pastor learns that the parents have not been consulted about the forthcoming marriage, or that after having been informed they reasonably refused to give their permission, then he must refer the matter to the local ordinary and await his decision. In the meantime, he is forbidden *sub gravi* to assist at the marriage.[5] As O'Donnell well states:

> It is true that the legislator commits to the individual pastor the right to decide this question, and only if the parents are reasonably unwilling must he consult the local ordinary. Consequently, the local ordinary is to estimate the gravity of the reasons, not in relation to the permission of the parties to contract marriage, but rather with a view to permitting the pastor to assist at the marriage in these circumstances. But in order to determine whether he should grant or refuse this permission to the pastor, it is necessary for him to readjudicate the reasons of the parents in opposing the marriage in the light of the child's reasons to contract this particular marriage. Therefore, the local ordinary is to reconsider the judgment of the pastor as to whether the unwillingness on the part of the parents is reasonable and just not only absolutely but also relatively to the marriage in question.[6]

In formulating his judgment, the local ordinary applies the same basic principles which the pastor employed. He must therefore diligently inquire into the reasons of the contracting parties for desiring to enter marriage, and also the reasons of the parents for opposing the marriage of their minor son or daughter. He receives this information from the form filled out by the pastor according to the Instruction of the Sacred Congregation of the Sacraments of June 29, 1941.[7]

---

4. Canons 1034 and 1020, §1.

5. Cf. O'Donnell, *The Marriage of Minors,* The Catholic University of America Canon Law Studies, n. 221 (Washington, D. C.: The Catholic University of America Press, 1945), pp. 113 and following.

6. *Op. cit.,* p. 174.

7. Allegatum III — Quaestiones seorsum proponendae parentibus (tutoribus) nupturientis aetate minoris (can. 1034), quando parocho certe non constet de absentia cuiusvis obstaculi ex parte ipsorum — *AAS,* XXXIII (1941), 315; Bouscaren, *The Canon Law Digest* (2 vols. and supplement through 1948, Milwaukee: Bruce, 1934, 1943, 1949), II, 272.

It is not sufficient that the parents have just and grave reasons for opposing the marriage. For the reasons of the parents must be considered in relation to those which their child has for wishing to enter the marriage.[8] If the local ordinary judges that the parental dissent is unreasonable, then he must permit the pastor to assist at the marriage. For it is the common doctrine that children may licitly enter a marriage to which their parents are unreasonably opposed.[9] This permission of the local ordinary suffices to suppress or overrule juridically the objections of the parents, and hence both the pastor and nupturients may proceed with the marriage.[10]

If, however, the local ordinary, after considering all the circumstances of the case, deems the parental refusal to be reasonable, he may then prohibit the marriage temporarily. In such a case he forbids the marriage, not precisely on account of the lack of parental consent, as if want of parental consent were a prohibitive impediment, but because of the reasons upon which the parental objections are based. In other words, the local ordinary judges that the reasons of the parents are founded on a just and canonical cause and outweigh the reasons which their minor son or daughter may have for desiring to enter the marriage.[11] For the Church is simply enforcing here a precept of the natural law, the duty of prudence and reverence to parents; it considers that precept important enough to require the intervention of the local ordinary to decide when this duty ceases to bind or when any contravention by the minor may be tolerated.[12]

However, if in a particular case the local ordinary foresees that refusal to permit the pastor to assist at a marriage would cause graver evils to arise, then in his prudence he should not prohibit the marriage. Thus, at times the local ordinary will be forced to permit the marriage even though the refusal of consent on the part of the

---

8. Cf. O'Donnell, *op. cit.*, pp. 156, 157.

9. Cappello, *De Matrimonio*, n. 187.

10. Canon 1034.

11. Wernz-Vidal, *Ius Matrimoniale*, n. 140; Gougnard, *loc. cit.*

12. Ayrinhac-Lydon, *Marriage Legislation in the New Code of Canon Law* (2. ed., New York: Benziger Bros., 1943), p. 51 (hereafter cited *Marriage Legislation*).

parents is reasonable and just. For in permitting the marriage, he will be choosing the lesser of two impending evils. While on the one hand there may be present the grave sin of disrespect and irreverence toward parents, on the other hand there may be the danger of the sin of scandal, of the celebration of a civil marriage, and of concubinage together with its series of grave sins. Since both of these evils cannot be effectively prevented, the natural law demands that the lesser of the two be permitted.[13] Hence, in such a case the local ordinary should allow the pastor to assist at the marriage notwithstanding the reasonable opposition on the part of the parents.

The local ordinary may prohibit the marriage of a minor whose parents are reasonably opposed to the marriage, even though the minor child is not his subject by reason of domicile or quasi-domicile. It is necessary and sufficient for the lawful and valid use of this power that the marriage is to be celebrated within the diocese of the local ordinary, and that the minor is actually present in the diocese at the time of the prohibition. The actual presence within the jurisdiction of the prohibiting ordinary is a necessary condition for the licit and valid prohibition of the marriage if the minor nupturient is a traveler or vagrant. If the minor is not a subject of the local ordinary and is not actually present within the diocese, the ordinary cannot prohibit the marriage. For under such circumstances any prohibition would be illicit, invalid, and devoid of all force.[14]

If the minor nupturient is his subject by reason of domicile or quasi-domicile, the local ordinary may prohibit the marriage even though the contracting parties are not present in his diocese at the time the prohibition is given. He may forbid the marriage even though it is to take place outside his diocese. His power to act thus endures as long as one or both of the contracting parties retain a domicile or quasi-domicile within the territorial limits of his diocese.[15]

---

13. Cappello, *De Matrimonio,* n. 192; Noldin-Schmitt, *Summa Theologiae Moralis iuxta Codicem Iuris Canonici* (27. ed., 3 vols., Oeniponte-Lipsiae: Sumptibus et Typis F. Rauch, 1940-1941), I, nn. 83-84 (hereafter cited Noldin-Schmitt).

14. Cappello, *ibid.,* n. 62.

15. Canons 1039 (§1) and 24.

Thus, even though the minor child has his own quasi-domicile in a diocese other than where his parents reside, the local ordinary of the parental domicile, and probably of the parental quasi-domicile also,[16] is competent to forbid the celebration of the marriage, even though it is to take place outside his diocese. For a minor necessarily shares the parental domicile[17] and, according to O'Donnell,[18] also the quasi-domicile.

In prohibiting the marriage of a minor the local ordinary may give the prohibition either directly to the pastor, forbidding him to assist at the marriage, or immediately to the nupturients themselves, obligating them to desist from their intention of entering this particular marriage. Or, if he deems it more effective, he may bind directly both the pastor and the parties by giving a double precept.

Although this prohibition of the local ordinary is not an impediment, it is a grave prohibition. Therefore, if the pastor and the parties disregard the prohibition, their action is gravely illicit, but the validity of the marriage is not affected thereby.[19]

In those cases in which, despite a reasonable and just parental refusal, the local ordinary permits the marriage in order to avert greater evils, he must act with the utmost prudence. For although the violation of the rightful parental authority is tolerated as the lesser evil, nevertheless the permitting of the marriage of a minor against the wishes of the parents is an action involving a certain amount of danger. The principal difficulty in permitting the celebration of a marriage which the parents oppose arises from the civil law, for all states in the United States have statutes dealing with the marriage of minors.[20]

---

16. Cf. O'Donnell, *op. cit.,* pp. 124-127. Note: It is also equally probable that the local ordinary of the parental quasi-domicile is not competent to forbid the celebration of the marriage in such a case.

17. Canon 93, §1. Emancipation takes place when one has completed one's twenty-first year. Cf. canon 88, §1.

18. *Loc. cit.*

19. Cappello, *De Matrimonio,* n. 62.

20. For a detailed treatment of the civil law on this matter, confer O'Donnell, *op. cit.,* pp. 195-208, 229-235. In this work the author observes that when a minor desires to contract marriage contrary to the will of his parents, three

When the parents are unreasonable in withholding their permission, the local ordinary should explain to them that in these circumstances the minor child has a right to enter marriage, that the Church must respect and uphold this right, and that therefore the parents also have a duty to respect this right of their child and to cease their unreasonable opposition. And if, in his prudence, the local ordinary judges it to be useful or necessary, he may impose on the parents a penal precept forbidding them to institute civil action in order to impede the marriage.[21]

Since the prohibition of the local ordinary endures only as long as the cause continues to exist,[22] it is evident that when the only cause of the prohibition is the lack of parental knowledge and consent, the parties are free to contract marriage when indisputable proof is offered that the parents now know of the marriage and give their consent. In other words, the prohibition ceases entirely by the very fact that the parents give their consent, and the parties have no obligation to await the decision of the local ordinary before the marriage can be lawfully celebrated. For by the operation of law the prohibition of the local ordinary ceases intrinsically and adequately when the cause or purpose of the prohibition no longer exists.[23]

---

types of civil law must be considered: (1) The civil ruling which requires parental consent for the marriages of persons under a certain age; (2) the civil statute demanding a license or certificate before the marriage can be celebrated; (3) the registration of the marriage in the public records of the state. He further observes that before the local ordinary advises the pastor to employ extraordinary remedies permitted by Canon Law, he should attempt to solve any difficulties either by an appeal to the civil courts or by advising marriage outside the jurisdiction of the particular state. In this way the civil effects of the marriage can be safeguarded. If neither of these remedies can be successfully employed, the local ordinary may resort to the solution offered in canons 1098 and 1104. Canon 1098 considers the celebration of a marriage before witnesses alone, while canon 1104 deals with the marriage of conscience.

---

21. Canon 2310.
22. Canon 1039, §1.
23. Cappello, *Summa,* I, n. 104; Cappello, *De Matrimonio,* n. 62; Payen, *op. cit.,* I, n. 589.

Therefore, if the sole reason of the local ordinary in forbidding the celebration of the minor's marriage against the reasonable will of the parents was to uphold and respect rightful parental authority, it is evident that as soon as the parents give their consent, the prohibition of the marriage ceases intrinsically and adequately. Consequently, the contracting parties are free to marry, and the pastor can lawfully assist at their marriage.

According to the law of the Code, the pastor is under no obligation to consult the local ordinary if the refusal of the parents is unreasonable. Canon 1034 prescribes that the ordinary be consulted only if the parents reasonably refuse to give their consent. According to the Code, therefore, if the parents are unreasonable in their opposition to the marriage, there is no obligation to refer the case to the local ordinary.

It may be asked, however, whether the local ordinary can demand that he be consulted in cases involving the marriage of minors even when the parents are unreasonable in their opposition. In other words, it may be asked whether the local ordinary can legislate to the effect that no pastor within his jurisdiction may lawfully assist at the marriage of a minor even though the parents are unreasonable in their opposition.

The legislative power of the bishop is expressly stated by the Code.[24] He may enact laws, both territorial and personal, and these laws are binding provided they are in accordance with the prescripts of the general law of the Code. Hence, his laws must be either in accord with (*secundum ius*) or beyond (*praeter ius*) the general law. Any regulation which is *contra ius* is by that very fact devoid of all force and need not be observed.[25] Thus a bishop cannot make a law which contradicts the general law of the Church. He cannot prohibit by law what is explicitly and indubitably conceded by the superior legislator; nor can he permit by his own law what is expressly prohibited by the higher authority.

The bishop, however, may rule regarding matters which lie outside the general law of the Church, and he may also adapt and partic-

24. Canon 335, §1.
25. Coronata, *Institutiones,* I, n. 394.

ularize the general law to the local conditions existing within his diocese.[26] He can adapt, he can particularize; but he cannot legislate contrary to the spirit of the universal law which he is adapting or particularizing. For canon 335, §1, requires that he exercise his legislative power *ad normam sacrorum canonum*. This phrase includes not merely the actual text of the general law, but also its spirit.[27] Therefore, legislation contrary to either element, be it the letter or the spirit of the law, is beyond the legislative competency of the bishop and consequently invalid.

In regard to the matter in question, it seems to be within the competency of the bishop to enact legislation requiring that he be consulted in all cases involving minors whose parents are opposed to the contemplated marriage — even when the opposition of the parents is unreasonable. Such legislation does not contradict any explicit ruling of the Code, for the Code does not explicitly declare that the pastor may assist at the marriage in those circumstances. Rather, the law is silent on this point. Neither in canon 1034 nor in any other canon does the Code explicitly concede to the pastor the right to assist at the marriage of minors without previously consulting the local ordinary when the parents are unreasonably opposed. Therefore, it is within the competency of the bishop to enact legislation requiring the pastor to refer the matter to him before assisting at the marriage of a minor even when the parents are unreasonable in their dissent.

In formulating such a law, the bishop is not in any way contradicting the law of the Code as it is expressed in canon 1034. Nor is he in any way violating the spirit of the law. For canon 1020, §3, obliges and directs the local ordinary to draw up appropriate norms for conducting prenuptial investigations, allowing him to adapt these rules to the particular needs and circumstances of his own diocese.[28]

---

26. Wernz-Vidal, *Ius Canonicum,* II, n. 599.

27. Roelker, "The Power to Enact Invalidating Laws," *The Jurist,* III (1943), 239.

28. Cf. S. C. de Sacr., instr., 29 iun. 1941 — *AAS,* XXXIII (1941), 298-299, nn. 2-3; Bouscaren, *op. cit.,* II, 253-254, nn. 2-3.

Therefore, if in the judgment of the bishop the necessity or utility of his diocese requires that he be consulted about minors intending to marry contrary to the unreasonable will of the parents, he may enact a law to this effect. Such a law would be valid, and pastors would be obliged to observe it.[29]

The particular needs of the diocese may require such a statute, especially in those places where the civil law of the locality upholds the parents in their opposition to the marriage, even though, canonically considered, their refusal is unjust.[30] In places wherein such a civil prescript is operative, the bishop should reserve to himself by diocesan law the right to determine under what conditions a marriage of this kind can be celebrated. For in these circumstances indiscriminate and injudicious assistance at the marriage of minors could result in great harm, not only to the pastors, but to the diocese and the Church at large. In so legislating, the bishop would not be acting contrary to the general law of the Church, but would merely be providing for the necessity and utility of his own diocese.[31]

---

29. Cappello, *De Matrimonio*, n. 153, 4.

30. In nearly all the states of the United States, the age below which the approbation of parents is needed is 21 for males and 18 for females. For a list of such states, and the variations in the age requirements in others, cf. Alford, *Jus Matrimoniale Comparatum* (New York: P. J. Kenedy and Sons, 1938), pp. 59-61, 207-209.

31. Some bishops of the United States in recent synods and provincial councils have ruled that the pastor must consult the ordinary when the parents refuse to give their consent. These laws do not distinguish between reasonable and unreasonable opposition on the part of the parents, and therefore bind even though the parents are unreasonable in their dissent. These laws have as their primary end the avoidance of a conflict in this matter with the civil law, and hence must bind even in cases wherein the parental refusal is canonically unjust. Cf. *Synodus Archidioecesis Sancti Francisci Secunda,* 14 oct. 1936 (San Francisco: Monitor Publishing Co., 1936), Cap. VII, n. 228; cf. *Synodus Dioecesana Fargensis Prima,* 29-30 sept. 1941 (Milwauchiae: Ex Typographia Bruce, 1941), Art. XIX, statutum 350, pp. 68-69; cf. *Acta et Decreta Concilii Provincialis Portlandensis in Oregon Quarti,* 10 sept. 1932, Cap. II, Art. VII, n. 298.

ARTICLE II. A PRUDENT DOUBT CONCERNING THE FREEDOM OF THE PARTY TO CONTRACT MARRIAGE

According to the present law of the Code, the right and obligation to determine the freedom of the parties desiring to contract marriage pertains primarily to the pastor who is competent to officiate at the marriage. For it is the duty of the competent pastor to investigate carefully whether there is any obstacle to the celebration of the marriage;[32] to admit the parties to the celebration of marriage;[33] and to assist at the marriage after having satisfied himself according to the norms required by law that the parties are free to marry.[34]

Under the present law, then, it is not ordinarily necessary that the freedom of parties desiring to contract marriage be evident to the local ordinary.[35] It is usually sufficient that the pastor concerned make an investigation and arrive at a conclusion concerning the freedom of the parties, without seeking the permission of the local ordinary to admit the nupturients to marriage.[36]

However, even under the present law of the Code it is sometimes necessary for the pastor to consult the local ordinary. In certain cases such consultation is necessary for obtaining full certitude about the

32. Canon 1020, §1.

33. Canon 1031, §3.

34. Canon 1097, §1, 1°.

35. It is worthy of note, however, that the instruction *Sacrosanctum* recommends that the pastor obtain permission or the *nihil obstat* from the diocesan Curia before he proceeds to assist at the marriage. Cf. S. C. de Sacr., instr., 29 iun. 1941 — *AAS,* XXXIII (1941), 299, n. 4a; Bouscaren, *op. cit.,* II, 255, n. 4a.

36. It was not thus in the earlier law. For in the common law prior to the Code it was in general necessary to prove the freedom of nupturients by means of a "*processus.*" This "process" involved, in addition to testimony regarding baptism and also confirmation in certain localities, the deposition of two witnesses testifying to the freedom of the nupturients in the prescribed form before the ordinary or his delegate; the investigation concerning the existence of impediments by the proper pastor; and the publication of the banns. At the completion of this process, if there was no evidence militating against the freedom of the parties, the local ordinary granted to the pastor the necessary permission to assist at the marriage. Cf. Cappello, *De Matrimonio,* n. 157.

freedom of the party concerned.[37] At other times it is necessary in order that the pastor may act legitimately according to law.[38] And in certain cases it is necessary for him to obtain permission to assist at a marriage.[39]

In cases wherein there are no positive arguments which tend to prove the freedom of the nupturient to marry, there remains a prudent doubt about a possible previous bond or an existing impediment. In such cases assuredly the pastor must consult the local ordinary before assisting at the marriage.[40] It is then the duty of the local ordinary to determine whether the marriage is to be immediately permitted, or prohibited for a time while further investigations are made.[41]

The decision of the local ordinary will depend, to a large extent, upon whether the prudent doubt about the party's freedom to marry is of a positive or only of a negative character. If the case is such that the doubt does not arise from any positive reason, but only from the fact that there are no positive arguments in favor of the nupturient's freedom, then the doubt may be considered a negative one. In such a case, if the party gives evidence of being trustworthy and testifies under oath concerning his freedom, and furthermore if there is no immediate hope of demonstrating his freedom by more conclusive arguments, then the ordinary should permit the marriage. For a nupturient should

37. Canons 1031, §1, 3°; 1023, §3.

38. Even though a previous marriage is certainly invalid, it is necessary to contact the local ordinary to obtain a declaration of nullity. For the competent judge is not the pastor, but the local ordinary. The latter can at times declare the nullity of the marriage by means of a definitive sentence. — Canons 1069, §2; 1960; 1990. Instruction of the Sacred Congregation of the Sacraments, *Provida,* 15 August, 1936, article 231 — *AAS,* XXVIII (1936), 359.

39. The permission of the local ordinary is necessary if one or both of the parties concerned be vagrants in the sense delineated in canon 91. — Canon 1032.

40. Canons 1097, §1, 1°; 1019, §1; 1023, §3; 1031, §1, 3°. Cf. Instruction of Sacred Congregation of Sacraments: "Ordinaries must be diligent in reminding pastors that they may not assist at marriages even under the pretext and for the purpose of keeping the faithful from unlawful concubinage, or of averting the scandal of so-called civil marriages, except upon satisfactory proof of the freedom of the parties to marry and with the observance of the requirements of law." — July 4, 1921; *AAS,* XIII, p. 348; Bouscaren, *op. cit.,* I, 497.

41. Cappello, *De Matrimonio,* n. 177.

not be forbidden to contract marriage either perpetually or for a long period of time merely because of a negative doubt as to his freedom.

Therefore, if there is no positive indication of a previous marriage or of any other impediment, but there are merely lacking positive arguments which clearly indicate the freedom of the party concerned, the ordinary is to be consulted. The ordinary is able to permit the marriage, especially if the nupturients are of upright and trustworthy character, and if they testify by means of a suppletory oath that they are free to marry.[42]

On the other hand, if there is present a truly positive doubt about the freedom of the parties concerned to contract marriage, the ordinary cannot permit the marriage until this doubt has in some way been removed. For the purpose of consulting the ordinary is not that he should immediately permit the marriage without dispelling the doubt.

Except only in the case of the doubtful impediment of impotence,[43] the local ordinary is not able to permit the marriage immediately unless the doubt concerns an impediment of purely ecclesiastical law, and the doubt can be obviated automatically by the law of the Church when it is a doubt of law, or by a dispensation *"ad cautelam"* when the doubt is one of fact.[44] Even in such a case, the ordinary may well impose a matrimonial ban pending ascertainment of the fact that there is only a doubt concerning the freedom of the parties.

Therefore, it is the function of the ordinary to determine whether the doubt is truly prudent and of sufficient importance to warrant further investigation. Thus, for instance, a vague and uncertain rumor cannot be said to constitute a prudent doubt when a diligent investigation has failed to produce any evidence to substantiate it.[45] On the other hand, common knowledge is usually sufficient to produce a truly prudent doubt.

Once the doubt has been established as being truly prudent, the ordinary should grant a dispensation *"ad cautelam"* if it is within his

42. Payen, *op. cit.,* I, n. 363; Wernz-Vidal, *Ius Matrimoniale,* n. 255, nota 53.

43. Canon 1068, §2.

44. Canon 15; Coronata, *De Matrimonio,* n. 101, a.

45. Coronata, *ibid.,* n. 102, a.

power to do so.[46] Even if he is unable to grant such a dispensation, he may nevertheless allow the marriage to be celebrated in certain cases,[47] while in others he must impose a matrimonial ban prohibiting the marriage until the prudent doubt has been resolved.[48]

In cases requiring the imposition of a matrimonial ban, the question is raised by the authors as to whether the testimony of one witness is sufficient justification for the imposition of the matrimonial ban even in those cases wherein the existence of the impediment cannot be proved in the external forum. It is certain that the marriage must be prohibited in such a case if the doubt concerns the impediment of a former bond or of consanguinity in the direct line or in the first degree of the collateral line.[49]

In regard to other impediments, it is the common opinion of the authors that the ordinary must prohibit the marriage if either he or the pastor is the one who is certain of the existence of the impediment.[50] If the impediment is revealed by a third party, the marriage should be prohibited if the third party is above all suspicion and testifies under oath.[51]

---

46. Where an impediment of ecclesiastical law only is concerned, the ordinary is able to grant a dispensation when there is a positive doubt of fact and the law is one from which the Holy See usually dispenses; and sometimes also in cases of impediments which are certain, in virtue of faculties contained in the common law or received in an indult.—Cf., v. g., canons 15; 1043; 1045.

47. If the doubtful impediment is of a prohibitive nature only, whether of the natural law or of the positive divine law or of the ecclesiastical law, the marriage may be permitted. For in cases of impediments which involve only the licitness of an act, one may invoke the general principle whereby a speculative probability concerning the licitness of an act becomes transformed by means of a reflex principle into a practical certainty of the licitness of the act. Cf. Coronata, *De Matrimonio,* n. 102, c; Noldin-Schmitt, I, n. 250.

48. If the doubt concerns an invalidating impediment, other than that of impotence, of either the natural law or the divine positive law, the marriage cannot be permitted. Cf. Cappello, *De Matrimonio,* n. 202.

49. Canons 1069, §2; 1076, §3.

50. This does not apply when the source of knowledge is sacramental confession or when the knowledge is obtained only by reason of the sacred ministry, for this makes the secret binding as an official secret. Cf. Cappello, *De Matrimonio,* n. 179.

51. Canon 1767; Payen, *op. cit.,* I, n. 493, 2, 3°.

In addition to those cases in which there is a prudent doubt concerning the freedom of the parties to contract marriage, the local ordinary must also be consulted about the marriage of vagrants. Except in a case of necessity, the pastor should never assist at the marriage of persons who are vagrants, as described in canon 91, unless after referring the matter to the ordinary of the place or to a priest delegated by him, he has obtained permission to assist.[52]

The purpose of this law is the attainment of greater certainty regarding the freedom of the party to marry. For since vagrants are less apt to be known, they might more easily attempt marriage while still bound by a former matrimonial bond. The law applies not only when both parties are vagrants, but even when only one of the nupturients comes under this classification.[53]

According to the law of the Code, vagrants are those who do not have either a domicile or a quasi-domicile.[54] Thus it would seem that those who have maintained residence in a diocese for a month but do not have a domicile or quasi-domicile either there or elsewhere are to be considered vagrants.[55]

Recourse to the ordinary is not necessary in cases of necessity; but even in such cases the pastor is unable to assist at the marriage unless he has conducted a thorough examination and is morally certain that the vagrant is free to marry.[56]

The local ordinary must prescribe, according to his prudence, a more searching examination of the freedom of the vagrant to marry, including the presentation of documents and the taking of suppletory oaths.[57] In the meantime he may impose a matrimonial ban prohibiting marriage until satisfactory proofs of the party's freedom to marry have been obtained.

52. Canon 1032.

53. Coronata, *De Matrimonio,* n. 107.

54. Canon 91.

55. Payen, *op. cit.,* III (altera editio, Zi-ka-wei: in Typographia T'ou-sè-wè, 1936), n. 496; Coronata, *loc. cit.;* Wernz-Vidal, *Ius Matrimoniale,* n. 541, nota 55.

56. Canon 1097, §1; Coronata, *loc. cit.*

57. *Loc. cit.*

Concerning this matter, the Sacred Congregation of the Sacraments warned that some marriages of laborers who had emigrated from Europe were to be considered as marriages of persons who had neither a domicile nor a quasi-domicile, at which the pastor was not to assist without having obtained due permission to do so from the ordinary of the place. Even if the persons in question were not vagrants, there was scarcely full freedom from doubt with reference to the existence of some impediment in the case of emigrants. Therefore, the Sacred Congregation forbade pastors to assist at such marriages except in a case of necessity, or especially in danger of death, without consulting the ordinary of the place.[58]

ARTICLE III. THE EMERGENCE OF SCANDAL

Although the concept of scandal can be said to belong primarily to the realm of moral theology, it is one which has very definite juridical implications. This is evident from the fact that it is mentioned explicitly in more than fifty canons of the Code. In addition, there are almost innumerable instances in which one must take note of it when seeking to effect a practical application of the law. The application of canon 1039, §1, the temporary prohibition of a particular marriage by the local ordinary, is one of these instances.[59]

In the light of the fact that the law of the Code is concerned with the right government of the Church of Christ and the salvation of the souls of His flock,[60] it is not surprising that it should contain many warnings and exhortations tending toward the preclusion of scandal. For Christ Himself indicated the true nature of scandal and emphasized its malice.[61] He realized it was not only a menace to the individual but a threat to the welfare of the common good of His Church.

---

58. Instruction of July 4, 1921, n. 4 — *AAS,* XIII (1921), 349.

59. Cappello, *De Matrimonio,* n. 62; Payen, *op. cit.,* I, n. 588; Gasparri, *Tractatus Canonicus de Matrimonio* (ed. nova, 2 vols., Romae: Typis Polyglottis Vaticanis, 1932), I, n. 230; Ayrinhac-Lydon, *Marriage Legislation,* n. 62.

60. Beste, *Introductio in Codicem,* p. 12.

61. Matth. 18:6 sq., 15-18.

Ecclesiastical jurisprudence indicates that the Church has been most solicitous down through the centuries in precluding scandal whenever possible and in extirpating it wherever it occurred. This policy of the Church is evident, even from earliest times, in both its administrative procedure and in its penal legislation.

The consistency with which, from the very beginning, the Church imposed the penalty of deposition on those who had been guilty of giving scandal[62] points to a definite meaning of scandal in penal legislation. Since scandal was always punished by means of a vindictive penalty, whose primary purpose was to repair the injured social order and to promote the common good,[63] it seems reasonable to conclude that in its penal legislation prior to the Council of Trent the Church considered scandal as being that which attacked the common good. While this is not essentially different from the meaning of scandal in moral theology, there does seem to be a distinction. For moral theology seems to be concerned with the element of scandal primarily as it has relation to the individual,[64] whereas ecclesiastical juridical science is concerned with scandal primarily only when it assumes such proportions as to threaten the common good.

---

62. Cf. I Council of Orange (441), cn. 23 — Bruns, *Canones Apostolorum et Conciliorum Saeculorum IV-VII* (2 vols., Berlini, 1839), II, 125 (hereafter cited Bruns); Council of Agde (506) — Hardouin, *Acta Conciliorum et Epistolae Decretales ac Constitutiones Summorum Pontificum* (12 vols., Parisiis, 1714-1715), II, 1003 (hereafter cited Hardouin); III Council of Orleans (538) — Hardouin, II, 1425; Council of Worms (868) — Mansi, XV, 871; c. 10, X, *de iudiciis,* II, 1; Jaffé, n. 17639; c. 4, X, *de excessibus praelatorum et subditorum,* IV, 31.

63. Cf. Council of Elvira (306), cn. 65 — Bruns, II, 10; Council of Ancyra (314), cc. 1-2 — Mansi, II, 514; Council of Arles (314), cn. 13 — Bruns, II, 108; Council of Neocæsarea (314/325), cn. 8 — Mansi, II, 540; IV Council of Carthage (398), cc. 48, 50, 56, 57 — Hardouin, I, 982; c. 25, D. L; *Glossa Ordinaria,* ad c. 25, D. L, s. v. *detrahendum est.*

64. Cf. St. Thomas Aquinas, *Summa Theologica,* IIa, IIae, q. 43, a. 1; Prümmer, *Manuale Theologiae Moralis secundum Principia S. Thomae Aquinatis* (10. ed., 3 vols., Barcelona: Editorial Herder, 1946), I, nn. 606-609; Noldin-Schmitt, II, nn. 102-104; Bucceroni, *Institutiones Theologiae Moralis,* I (4. ed., Romae, 1900), 419-421; Aertnys-Damen, *Theologia Moralis,* Vol. I (14. ed., Romae: Marietti, 1944), nn. 377-382.

In addition to the part which scandal played in penal legislation, it was also a very important element in purely administrative matters. The Decretals indicate that it was a very popular cause for dispensation from the positive law.[65] And Reiffenstuel further emphasized the juridical pertinence of scandal by indicating that the utility of many was to be preferred to the welfare of the individual, and that in order to extinguish scandal and maintain peace, the precepts of the law were to be relaxed.[66]

It is not surprising, therefore, that the Decretals indicate that the danger of scandal was a common cause, not only for granting dispensations,[67] but also for restricting the rights of certain persons in contracting marriage.[68] For such a method of procedure shows that the Church was interested in the common good and in its own general welfare even when it necessitated the restraint of the right of the individual. Thus it was that custom or scandal impeded the right of persons to marry, even of those who were otherwise free to do so;[69] that the ordinary or his judge was to impose a matrimonial ban on a

65. Sandeus (1444-1503), *Commentaria in Quinque Libros Decretalium* (5 vols. in 3, Venetiis, 1570), c. 2, X, *de praescriptionibus,* II, 26 (hereafter cited *Commentaria*).

66. "Bonum commune praeferendum est privato. Propter scandalum relaxanda ac dimittenda sunt iura. . . . Ratio est quia bonum publicum debet praeferri privato, can. 35, caus. 7, q. 1, ibi: 'Nam plurimorum utilitas unius utilitati aut voluntati praeferenda est'; et ad extinguendum scandalum atque pro bono pacis relaxanda sunt iuris praecepta." — *Ius Canonicum Universum,* tit. *de rerum permutatione,* Lib. III, tit. 19, n. 39.

67. C. 6, X, *de consanguinitate et affinitate,* IV, 14; Potthast, n. 4820; Migne, III, 914. ". . . secunda causa propter scandalum evitandum unde hodie et quotidie Papa dispensat inter consanguineos propter bonum pacis futurum, vel scandalum evitandum et haec causa sufficiens est nedum post matrimonium contractum, sed ante quia propter scandalum recedendum est a dispositione iuris positivi." — Panormitanus, *Commentaria,* tit. *de consanguinitate et affinitate,* Lib. IV, tit. 14, c. 6, n. 2.

68. C. 27, X, *de sponsalibus et matrimoniis,* IV, 1; c. 1, X, *de cognatione spirituali,* IV, 11; c. 3, X, *de cognatione spirituali,* IV, 11; c. 3, X, *de consanguinitate et affinitate,* IV, 14.

69. "Nota . . . consuetudo sive scandalum praejudicat iuri in matrimoniis, ut personas legitimas ad contrahendum faciat illegitimas." — *Glossa Ordinaria,* ad c. 3, X, *de consanguinitate et affinitate,* IV, 14, s. v. *casus.*

marriage if scandal was to be feared from it;[70] that because of scandal a marriage should be impeded even if otherwise it was legitimate;[71] and that parties related by compaternity could intermarry if such was the custom, but could not if custom did not warrant it — for a custom which if it had not been observed would have given rise to scandal was to be observed even in violation of the law.[72]

Moreover, in ecclesiastical jurisprudence, the word "scandal" was used in the broadest sense of the term. Thus, in the Decretals it was used to include bewilderment, shock, or wonderment which might cause criticism of the Church and a relaxing of its discipline.[73] Sanchez further explained that it also included the notions of enmities, quarrels, and dissensions which arise among relatives. He called attention to the fact that the actual presence or existence of scandal was not required, but that the reasonable fear that scandal would become a reality in the future was sufficient cause for action.[74]

Reiffenstuel included *"extinctio litis," "gravis inimicitia,"* and *"conservatio pacis"* among the causes reducible to a consideration under the notion of scandal, and considered action necessary in these cases because failure to act would be detrimental to the common good.[75]

---

70. "Scandalum si vehementer timetur ex contractu matrimonii, potest et debet judex matrimonium interdicere . . . ex quo potes inferre quod ubi inter aliquas parentelas scandalum vehementer timetur ex contractu matrimonii, potest et debet iudex interdicere matrimonium." — Panormitanus, *op. cit.*, tit. *de sponsalibus et matrimoniis*, Lib. IV, tit. 1, c. 27, n. 4.

71. "Solutio potest dici, quod hoc locum habet in matrimonio contrahendo, ut propter scandalum impediatur matrimonium quod alias legitimum est." — *Glossa Ordinaria*, ad c. 1, X, *de cognatione spirituali*, IV, 11, s. v. *nisi consuetudo quae scandalum.*

72. "Consuetudo facit personas legitimas vel illegitimas ad contrahendum. . . . Et intellige de tali consuetudine, quae scandalum generaret nisi fuerit observata." — *Glossa Ordinaria*, ad c. 3, X, *de cognatione spirituali*, IV, 11, s. v. *casus* et *consuetudo.*

73. *Glossa Ordinaria*, ad c. 6, X, *de clericis conjugatis*, III, 3, s. v. *repugnet;* c. 14, X, *de homicidio voluntario vel casuali*, V, 12.

74. Sanchez, *De Matrimonio*, Lib. VIII, Disp. XIX, nn. 9-10.

75. *Ius Canonicum Universum, Appendix de Dispensatione super Impedimentis Matrimonii et Petendi Debitum*, Sec. III, nn. 72-75.

Schmalzgrueber[76] and Wernz[77] list the fears of grave quarrels, enmities, and scandals among the causes which justify and even require the prohibition of particular marriages by the local ordinary.

Thus, it seems reasonable to conclude that in ecclesiastical jurisprudence prior to the Code the existence or the fear of scandal was a just and sufficient cause for the prohibition of a particular marriage; that the term "scandal" was used in the very broad sense to include bewilderment, shock, and wonderment which might cause criticism to the Church, and also to designate enmities, quarrels, and dissensions among the faithful; that the local ordinary was to be the judge of the existence or the danger of scandal; and that the particular malice of scandal was to be found in the fact that it was a threat to the common good.

According to the law of the Code, the local ordinary may prohibit a particular marriage "for a just cause."[78] Among the just causes enumerated by the commentators, the existence or also the fear of scandal holds a prominent place.[79] Moreover, such things as "*graves inimicitiae*,"[80] "*graves discordiae*,"[81] "*gravia incommoda*,"[82] and "*similia*"[83] are likewise mentioned. It seems, therefore, that also in the law of the Code the term "scandal," as used to designate a just cause for the temporary prohibition of a particular marriage, is to be interpreted in a broad sense. It therefore includes the notions of enmities, quarrels, and dissensions among the faithful, and even bewilderment, shock, and wonderment when these are detrimental to the welfare of the Church. Canon 1039, §1, makes it quite evident that the local ordinary is to be the judge of the existence or the danger of such scandal in each individual case.

---

76. *Ius Ecclesiasticum Universum*, Lib. IV, tit. 16, n. 2.

77. *Ius Matrimoniale*, n. 599.

78. Canon 1039, §1.

79. Payen, *De Matrimonio*, I, n. 588; Cappello, *De Matrimonio*, n. 62; Gasparri, *De Matrimonio*, I, n. 230; Ayrinhac-Lydon, *Marriage Legislation*, n. 62.

80. Payen, *loc. cit.*

81. Payen, *loc. cit.;* Cappello, *loc. cit.;* Gasparri, *loc cit.*

82. "... verus timor ne e matrimonio oriantur gravia incommoda." — Payen, *op. cit.*, III, n. 586.

83. Cappello, *loc. cit.*

The local ordinary is given wide discretionary authority in dealing with cases involving scandal. In all probability no two cases will present exactly the same difficulties. It is the duty of the local ordinary, as shepherd of his diocese, to avert all that constitutes a danger to his flock. For the good of his fold it may sometimes be necessary to restrict the rights of certain individuals in relation to the sacrament of matrimony.

At times he may successfully avert the danger to the common good by restricting only the circumstances of the marriage — for instance, by forbidding solemnity or publicity relative to the marriage; or by prohibiting the marriage in that territory where the parties are well known. At other times it may be necessary to forbid the marriage itself until the danger of scandal can be obviated in some other way. The solution in each individual case is left to the prudent judgment of the local ordinary. The power enabling him to take the necessary action is granted by the Code in canon 1039, §1.

ARTICLE IV. A SINFUL INTENTION TO ABUSE THE MARITAL RIGHT

In recent years one of the most serious threats in married life to both the sanctity of the individual and the general welfare of society has been the ever-increasing use of contraceptive measures. Although it is evident that the reproductive endowments of human nature exist primarily for a social objective, namely, the propagation and conservation of mankind, the whole spirit of our age tends toward regarding marriage as intended primarily for the pleasure of the individual. As a result, the vice of contraception has spread throughout our entire society.

Contraception in all its forms is a violation of the Sixth Commandment.[84] Inasmuch as it is directly opposed to nature, it is seriously sinful.[85] For in contraception man completely perverts the order of

84. Noldin-Schmitt, *De Sexto Praecepto et De Usu Matrimonii* (31. ed., Oeniponte-Lipsiae: Sumptibus et Typis F. Rauch, 1940), n. 73 (hereafter cited *De Sexto Praecepto;* Davis, *Moral and Pastoral Theology,* Vol. IV (fourth edition, revised and enlarged, New York: Sheed and Ward, 1943), 260-261.

85. Chrétien, *De Matrimonio Praelectiones* (ed. 2., Metis: Typis Imprimierie du Journal "Le Lorrain," 1937), n. 243 (hereafter cited *De Matrimonio*).

nature and acts contrary to the will of the Creator.[86] Pleasure becomes an end in itself rather than a means to a higher end, as intended by God. The social purpose of the marital right is disregarded, and man makes it exclusively individual. He not only seeks this pleasure as an end in itself, but actually takes deliberate steps to make certain that the basic purpose of this pleasure, the propagation of the race, shall not be attained.[87]

The Church has proclaimed the intrinsic evil of these practices, and its condemnation of such sins has been an uninterrupted Christian tradition.[88] Since the serious immorality of these practices is patently manifest, no reason can change what is in itself contrary to nature and make it conformable to nature and right.[89]

The specific inordination of the act lies in the fact that it is opposed to the primary end of marriage.[90] For contraception directly and positively excludes generation in the very act from which it should naturally be the result. Since the conjugal act is destined primarily by nature

---

86. "Quoties adeo contravenitur modo naturali concubitus ut ex natura facti generatio subsequi nequeat, est peccatum letale contra naturam: quia frustratur semen in fine ad quem natura ipsum destinavit." — Sanchez, *op. cit.,* Lib. IX, Disp. XX, n. 1 sq.

87. "Huic enim fini [bona societatis humanae] positive adversatur onanista, cum, contra ipsam matrimonii institutionem, completam voluptatem veneream, ex seminis effusione ortam, seiungat a fine suo naturali, id est a generatione prolis et generis humani propagatione. . . . In eo casu actus speciei fit, contra ordinem totius facultatis generativae, actus personae individuae." — Payen, *De Matrimonio,* II (altera editio, Zi-ka-wei: in Typographia T'ou-sè-wè, 1936), n. 2099.

88. Pius XI, litt. encycl. *Casti connubii,* 31 dec. 1930: ". . . christiana doctrina iam inde ab initio tradita neque umquam intermissa . . ." — *AAS,* XXII (1930), 560. Cf. Romans, I: 24-27; Augustine, *De Coniugiis Adulterinis,* II, 12 — *MPL,* XL, 479; S. C. S. Off., 21 maii 1851, as quoted by Heylen, *Tractatus de Matrimonio* (ed. 9., Mechliniae: H. Dessain, 1945), p. 418 (hereafter cited *De Matrimonio*); S. C. S. Off., 6 aprilis 1853, ad I, as quoted by Heylen, *De Matrimonio,* p. 418.

89. Pius XI, litt. encycl. *Casti connubii,* 31 dec. 1930: "Nulla profecto ratio ne gravissima quidem efficere potest, ut quod intrinsice est contra naturam, id cum natura congruum et honestum fiat." — *AAS,* XXII (1930), 559.

90. "Omnis actus luxuriae praeter commixtionem maris et feminae dicitur esse contra naturam inquantum non est proportionatus generationi." — Thomas Aquinas, *Opera Omnia,* XIII (Parisiis, 1875), *De Malo,* Qu. XV, art. 1, p. 258.

for the begetting of children, those who in exercising it deliberately frustrate its natural power and purpose sin against nature and commit a deed which is shameful and intrinsically vicious.[91]

This is true even though they are man and wife. For although the marriage bond bestows upon the parties concerned the right to the marital act, it bestows it upon them only insofar as the act is performed in a natural manner, that is, in such a way that it is of itself suited for the begetting of children.[92]

In addition to the fact that it is contrary to nature, the practice of contraception defeats the secondary ends of marriage, for it is opposed to the mutual help of the spouses one to the other,[93] and to the allaying of concupiscence.[94]

Furthermore, the positive preclusion in the conjugal act of its natural purpose of promoting the good of the species, and the relegation of this act to the position of a mere convenience for the parties concerned cannot but result in dire consequences to society in general. Not only is it detrimental to the common good,[95] but it actually tends

---

91. Pius XI, litt. encycl. *Casti connubii,* 31 dec. 1930: "Cum actus coniugii suapte natura proli generandae sit destinatus, qui, in eo exercendo, naturali hac eum vi atque virtute de industria destruunt, contra naturam agunt et turpe quid atque intrinsice inhonestum operantur." — *AAS,* XXII (1930), 559.

92. "... nec eam malitiam aufert status coniugalis, cum vinculum coniugale legitimet quidem, uti vidimus, copulam inter coniuges admissam, sed eam solam quae per se ordinata existit ad finem generationis; ad hanc etiam solam copulam ius acquiritur ab uno coniuge erga compartem." — De Smet, *De Matrimonio,* n. 240.

93. "Ideo mutuo adiutorio adversatur quia extinguit mutuam reverentiam, mutuum amorem eo nomine dignum, mulieris dignitatem." — Payen, *De Matrimonio,* III, n. 2099.

94. "Nonnisi actu consummato et mutuo amore prolis quae nata est, aut saltem, vi actus externi, nasci potest, sedatur concupiscentia." — *Loc. cit.*

95. " . . . adversatur . . . praesertim bono societatis humanae" — Noldin-Schmitt, *De Sexto Praecepto,* n. 73. "Vitium illud non tantum moribus Christianis ac ipsi legi naturali in corde uniuscuiusque hominis insculptae summopere repugnat, sed etiam, docente experientia, tam pro individuis, quam pro familiis atque humano genere, pessimas sequelas secum trahit. Ubicumque vigit, nedum aedificentur domus atque humana societas amplificetur et roboretur, validis membris vacuantur familiae, enervatur pactum matrimoniale et coniuges animi doloribus, remorsu conscientiae, corporalibusque miseriis cruciari solent." — *Instructiones EE. Belgii,* as quoted by Gougnard, *De Matrimonio,* p. 255, nota 3.

to the very destruction of society itself.[96] Specifically, the practice of contraception leaves in its wake an increasing number of abortions and fornications;[97] it sounds the death knell of the dignity of the family and causes the overthrow of public morality;[98] and it results in a decreasing birth rate which slowly but surely spells doom for society itself.[99]

Since the practice of contraception results in such grave harm to both the individual and society, and since it is manifestly opposed to God's law, it is not surprising that Pius XI warned those entrusted with the care of souls that they must not allow the faithful to remain in error regarding this most serious law of God; and that if any pastor of souls should be the cause of some members of his flock falling into this error or remaining in it because of his untimely silence, he would be required to render an account to Almighty God for the neglect of his duty.[100]

---

96. "... vergit in destructionem generis humani." — Davis, *Moral and Pastoral Theology,* IV, p. 261; "... haec ratio utendi matrimonio est de se destructiva societatis." — Cappello, *De Matrimonio,* n. 820.

97. De Smet, *De Matrimonio,* n. 240; Gougnard, *De Matrimonio,* p. 256.

98. *Loc. cit.*

99. "Pro societate onanismus est gravissimum malum: est enim praecipua causa denatalitatis, sicque lenta mors societatis. Ob liberorum numerum minutum natalitas propior fit mortalitati quae, etsi ob progressus hygienicos minor effecta, tamen indefinite minui nequit, et mox mortalitatem adaequat et superat, ita ut plures sint arcae mortuorum quam neonatorum curae." — Chrétien, *De Matrimonio,* n. 243.

100. Pius XI, litt. encycl. *Casti connubii,* 31 dec. 1930: "Sacerdotes igitur ... aliosque qui curam animarum habent, pro suprema Nostra auctoritate et omnium animarum salutis cura, admonemus, ne circa gravissimam hanc Dei legem fideles sibi commissos errare sinant, et multo magis, ut ipsi se ab huiusmodi falsis opinionibus immunes custodiant, neve in iis ullo modo conniveant. Si quis vero ... animarum Pastor, quod Deus avertat, fideles sibi creditos aut in hos errores ipsemet induxerit, aut saltem sive approbando sive dolose tacendo in iis confirmarit, sciat se Supremo Iudici Deo de muneris proditione severam redditurum esse rationem." — *AAS,* XXII (1930), 560.

This same Pontiff also declared that legitimately constituted authority has not only the right but the duty to restrict, to prevent, and to punish base unions which are opposed to reason and to nature.[101]

In accordance with this obligation of the legitimately constituted authority to restrict and prevent base unions which are opposed to reason and to nature, the Church charges bishops with the duty of giving to the pastors subject to them appropriate norms for conducting prenuptial investigations so as to ascertain that there is no obstacle to Christian marriage.[102]

In addition, it has been suggested that when the bishop deems it advisable the pastor shall intimate to both parties that he is sure that they both wish to contract marriage according to Catholic teaching, as it is done by all the faithful, that is, as an indissoluble relationship, proper for the procreation of children, without any contrary intention or condition.[103]

In compliance with this instruction, and in accordance with the control granted them by the Code over the specific form of the prenuptial investigations,[104] certain ordinaries have introduced into prenuptial questionnaires and antenuptial guarantees the wording of a promise to be given by both parties to the effect that they will lead a married life in conformity with the teachings of the Church regarding birth control, realizing fully the attitude of the Catholic Church in this regard.

Once this investigation has served its purpose and brought to light an intention to abuse the marital right by contraceptive methods,

---

101. Pius XI, litt. encycl. *Casti connubii,* 31 dec. 1930: "Exinde iam constat legitimam quidem auctoritatem iure pollere atque adeo cogi officio coercendi, impediendi, puniendi turpia coniugia, quae rationi ac naturae adversantur." — *AAS,* XXII (1930), 542.

102. S. C. de Sacr., instr., 29 iun. 1941: "Ecclesia onus commisit animarum Praesulibus impertiendi parochis sibi subiectis idoneas normas pro investigationibus sedulo et opportuno tempore peragendis, ne matrimonio ineundo aliquid obstet." — *AAS,* XXXIII (1941), 298; Bouscaren, *The Canon Law Digest,* II, 253.

103. *Ibid.,* Appendix, Exhibit I, n. 15 — *AAS,* XXXIII (1941), 312; Bouscaren, *ibid.,* 268.

104. "Ordinarii loci est peculiares normas pro huismodi parochi investigatione dare." — Canon 1020, §3.

measures must be taken to induce the parties to retract this sinful intention.[105] Usually the pastor who is performing the prenuptial examination can do no more than exhort the parties to retract their sinful intention. In those cases in which the exhortation is to no avail, he cannot, on his own authority, refuse to assist at the marriage when the parties are non-public sinners.[106] And generally such persons will come under the classification of non-public sinners.

Only rarely will the sinful intention on the part of one or both of the contracting parties be publicly known, for example, by reason of public statements, or membership or affiliation with leagues or associations which promote birth control and unnaturally planned parenthood. In such cases, unless the sinful intention is retracted publicly by means of a public approach to sacramental confession,[107] the pastor may not assist at the marriage unless there is a grave reason for so doing, in which case he should if possible consult the ordinary.[108]

However, in the ordinary cases in which the sinful intention of the parties is not publicly known, the pastor can only exhort the parties to retract their intention of abusing the marital right and to receive the sacrament of penance. But he cannot make prenuptial confession obligatory in such cases. For this would be demanding more than the Church prescribes. The Church merely declares that the pastor should earnestly exhort the contracting parties to go to confession and receive Holy Communion before their marriage.[109] Thus in the case

---

105. Pius XI, litt. encycl. *Casti connubii,* 31 dec. 1930: "Si . . . animarum pastor . . . fideles sibi creditos . . . dolose tacendo in iis [erroribus] confirmarit, sciat se Supremo Iudici Deo de muneris proditione severam redditurum esse rationem." — *AAS,* XXII (1930), 560.

106. Cappello, *De Matrimonio,* n. 332.

107. "Opus est ut *publice* constet de re vel per actum natura publicum, e. g., per accessum ad tribunal poenitentiae palam in ecclesia, vel per divulgationem." — Cappello, *loc. cit.*

108. "Si publicus peccator aut censura notorie innodatus prius ad sacramentalem confessionem accedere aut cum ecclesia reconciliari recusaverit, parochus eius matrimonio ne assistat, nisi gravis urgeat causa, de qua, si fieri possit, consulat Ordinarium." — Canon 1066.

109. ". . . eosdemque vehementer adhortetur ut ante matrimonii celebrationem sua peccata diligenter confiteantur, et sanctissimam Eucharistiam pie recipiant." — Canon 1033.

of such non-public sinners, the pastor, on his own authority, can neither refuse to assist at the marriage nor demand prenuptial confession as a prerequisite condition to his assistance.

However, since the parties concerned intend to commit a crime of no small gravity by violating the law of God and abusing the marital right,[110] it is clearly the responsibility of the local ordinary to see to it that they do not enter marriage with such a sinful intention. For the Holy See, mindful of the grave evils which flow from illicit and invalid marriages, has charged the local ordinaries with the duty of removing all danger of transgression in this regard and ensuring the celebration of marriages in such a fashion as become the dignity and sanctity of the sacrament.[111]

The upholding of God's law, the right use of the natural faculties, the salvation of individuals, and the welfare of society all depend upon the local ordinary's taking prompt and efficient action in these cases. Therefore, in accordance with the duty entrusted to him by the Holy See, the local ordinary may use the power given him in canon 1039, §1, in order to prohibit the marriage of persons intending to abuse the marital right until they can be shown the intrinsic evil of contraceptive practices and induced to retract their sinful intention in this regard.

---

110. S. C. de Sacr., instr., 29 iun. 1941: "Neminem latet gravem in sacramentum iniuriam committere, ideoque nec levi commaculari crimine, nupturientes qui ad matrimonium accedant haud servatis praeceptis ab Ecclesia naviter statutis ut christianae nuptiae licite, et praesertim valide, ineantur aptaeque praeterea evadant ad uberes sacramenti fructus comparandos." — *AAS,* XXXIII (1941), 297-298; Bouscaren, *op. cit.,* II, 253.

111. S. C. de Sacr., instr., 29 iun. 1941: "Haec Sacra Congregatio, gravissima incommoda quae ex illicitis atque irritis nuptiis eveniunt prae oculis habens, locorum Ordinarios deprecatur ut, pro sua pastorali sollicitudine, cum parochis traditas cautelas communicent omnique cura advigilent ut exsecutioni mandentur, canonicasque poenas infligere ne omittant . . . quo tutius nuptiarum rectae celebrationi prospiciatur, cuiusvis offensionis periculo remoto, prouti sacramenti matrimonii dignitatem et sanctitatem decet." — *AAS,* XXXIII (1941), 306-307; Bouscaren, *op. cit.,* II, 264.

Article V. The Presence of a Communicable Social Disease Unknown to the Other Party

The dire consequences of the ailments known as venereal diseases and their prevalence throughout our land have resulted in an extensive campaign against them. One of the methods employed in this campaign has been "eugenic legislation," the passing of laws which forbid persons to marry as long as they are suffering from a venereal disease. For the detection of syphilis thirty-six states now require premarital examination, including a blood test.[112]

The laws of some of these states declare the marriage of a diseased person null and void, at least when he has not informed the other party of his condition; the laws in other states merely forbid the marriage of such persons.[113] "Most premarital examination laws prevent the marriage of a person who has syphilis in a communicable stage. After treatment has rendered a person permanently noninfectious, that person can marry. With modern methods this means that the premarital law does not permanently bar marriage of persons having syphilis, but only requires postponement."[114]

It is therefore quite evident that many states have made the presence of a communicable social disease an impediment to marriage. By forbidding marriage to baptized persons afflicted with venereal disease, these states have usurped for themselves jurisdiction which belongs to the Church alone. Even if they intended to bind only unbaptized persons, the legality of such measures might still be questioned from the standpoint of the natural law.[115] But since they intend to bind both baptized and unbaptized alike, the laws of these states forbidding marriage to those afflicted with venereal diseases must be regarded in respect to the baptized as transgressions of the order of authority as established by God. For only the Church can establish impediments, whether diriment or prohibitive, for baptized persons.[116]

---

112. Clarke, "The Conquest of Venereal Disease," *Hygeia* (Chicago, Ill., 1923-), XXVII (1949), 201.

113. Alford, *Jus Matrimoniale Comparatum*, pp. 148-154.

114. Clarke, *loc. cit.*

115. De Smet, *De Matrimonio*, nn. 422-424.

116. Canon 1038, §2.

It is true that the State may legislate for the merely civil effects of the marriages of baptized persons.[117] Thus the State may at times indirectly prevent marriages — even those of baptized persons — when the use of its proper civil rights entails as a consequence that some persons are rendered incapable, either permanently or temporarily, of marrying.[118] Furthermore, the State may use its legislative and coercive powers regarding what is prescribed or forbidden by the natural law concerning marriage, insofar as violations of this law are detrimental to the welfare of civil society. Its power in this regard extends to both the baptized and the unbaptized.[119]

But this power of the State over baptized persons is limited to matters prescribed or forbidden by the natural law according to the teachings of the Catholic Church; for it belongs only to the supreme authority of the Church to declare authentically when the divine law impedes or invalidates marriage.[120] And according to the teachings of the Catholic Church it is not against the natural law for one afflicted with a communicable social disease to marry.

All Catholic moralists admit that there is a grave violation of the natural law when a diseased person marries one who is healthy and

117. Canon 1016.

118. Francis J. Connell, C. SS. R., "May the State Forbid Marriage Because of a Social Disease?" *The Ecclesiastical Review,* XCIX (1938), 510-511. Father Connell therein explains that "such an exercise of civil power takes place when the State . . . segregates those afflicted with a contagious disease in order to prevent its spread. Underlying this doctrine is the well-known moral principle that a bad effect may at times be permitted as a concomitant or a consequence of a good effect. In this instance the bad effect is the restriction of the natural right to marry. . . . It is to be noted that the State's reason for employing its power in such a case must be proportionate to the grave inconvenience inflicted on those inhibited."

119. Connell, *loc. cit.;* "In specie, quod spectat crimina, legem matrimonialem Ecclesiae simul ac ordinem status civilis laedentia, uti sunt adulterium et abortus, potest illa [status civilis] iudicare ac punire; non posset tamen illas causas tractare in ordine praecise ad matrimonium, puta quoad consortium vitae interdicendum vel suspendendum." — De Smet, *op. cit.,* n. 427.

120. Canon 1038, §1.

is not aware of the other's condition.[121] But ecclesiastical jurisprudence upholds the right of a person with a communicable disease to marry as long as this condition is known to the other party and the other party is nevertheless willing. This was true under the decretal law,[122] and remained unchanged prior to the Code.[123]

The Code makes no mention of venereal disease as an impediment to marriage.[124] The question is a moral rather than a canonical question. For a person who is afflicted with a terrible and highly contagious disease, such as syphilis, is forbidden by the natural law of charity to marry without informing the other party of his condition.[125] But once he has made his condition known, and the other party is still willing, there is no impediment to such a marriage from the natural law.[126]

---

121. Connell, *op. cit.,* p. 514. Cf. Payen, *op. cit.,* I, nn. 537, 540; Gury-Tummolo-Iorio, *Compendium Theologiae Moralis* (ed. 5., Neapoli: M. D'Auria, 1934-1935), I, n. 403 bis; Iorio, *Theologia Moralis* (3 vols., Neapoli: M. D'Auria, 1946-1947), II, n. 187.

122. "... leprosi autem si continere nolunt et aliquam quae sibi nubere velit invenerint, liberum est eis ad matrimonium convolare." — C. 2, X, *de coniugio leprosorum,* IV, 8; "Si leprosi continere nolunt, bene possunt contrahere matrimonium, dummodo inveniant qui ipsos accipere velint." — *Glossa Ordinaria,* ad c. 2, X, *de coniugio leprosorum,* IV, 8, s. v. *casus.* Note: Although this title of the Decretals deals explicitly with the disease of leprosy, it applies likewise "quovis alio morbo contagioso ... uti est morbus gallicus." — Schmalzgrueber, *Ius Ecclesiasticum Universum,* Lib. IV, tit. 8, n. 3. Cf. also Wernz, *Ius Matrimoniale,* n. 253.

123. "... nuptiae leprosis non sunt prohibitae, cum de prohibitione nuspiam iuris aliquis textus extet, sed potius de licentia ... ergo lepra non impedit a matrimonio contrahendo." — Schmalzgrueber, *ibid.,* n. 5; "Lepra nec dirimens nec impediens est impedimentum matrimonii, non tantum si ambo sunt leprosi, sed etiam quando unus tantum leprosus est; dummodo inveniat qui ei nubere velit." — Reiffenstuel, *Ius Canonicum Universum* (5 vols. in 6, Romae, 1831-1834), Lib. IV, tit. 8, n. 2; cf. also Wernz, *Ius Matrimoniale,* n. 256.

124. Cf. canons 1035-1080.

125. Bouscaren-Ellis, *Canon Law* (Milwaukee: The Bruce Publishing Co., 1948), p. 473.

126. "... altera pars monita iam et edocta de tali morbo existente in comparte, nihilominus consentiat, licebit eis matrimonio uti, et si nondum contraxerint, illud contrahere: scienti enim et volenti non fit iniuria." — Iorio, *loc. cit.;* cf. also Gury-Tummolo-Iorio, *loc. cit.*

Therefore, the civil authority has no power to prescribe a medical examination for baptized persons in such wise that if this condition is not fulfilled, marriage is forbidden to them. For when the State takes legislative or coercive action regarding the supernatural contract of marriage in the case of baptized persons, or determines the conditions required of those who wish to make the contract, the State has exceeded the bounds of the merely civil effects of marriage.[127] By such action it has established, directly or indirectly, an impediment, either diriment or prohibitive; and to establish such an impediment for baptized persons is entirely beyond the power of the State.[128]

Of course, in those states in which eugenic laws have been passed, Catholics must in prudence conform to the statutes. Yet one likewise must recognize that according to Catholic doctrine such laws do not bind baptized persons in conscience, but are rather an infringement on the authority of the Church and an unwarranted restriction of the natural right to marry.[129]

Nevertheless, the fact remains that a person who is afflicted with a terrible and highly contagious disease is forbidden by the natural law of charity to marry without informing the other party of his condition.[130] This prohibition of the natural law remains until such

---

127. Connell, *op. cit.*, p. 512.

128. "Utrum potestas civilis saltem praescribere possit nupturientium examen seu inspectionem medicam? Quoad baptizatos, nequit tale examen praescribere ita, ut non servata hac conditione, matrimonium ipsis esset interdictum vel non agnosceretur civiliter . . . sic enim directe vel saltem indirecte impedimentum dirimens vel prohibens constitueret, ad quod prorsus incompetens est." — Aertnys-Damen, *Theologia Moralis,* II, n. 636.

129. Connell, *op. cit.*, p. 515.

130. "Iustitia, adeoque ius naturale, graviter prohibet, quin tamen illud irritet, matrimonium in compartem iniustum, id est matrimonium quod nequeat iniri sine gravi iniuria alteri parti illata. Huiusmodi est, ut patet, matrimonium contractum, cum parte *non praemonita,* a parte quae morbo valde contagioso, et potissimum syphilide, actu laborat." — Payen, *De Matrimonio,* I, n. 537; "Qui tali igitur morbo laborat, cavere debet tum ex caritate tum ex iustitia, ne ipse sit causa cur proximus eodem inficiatur vel periculo exponatur illum contrahendi; alteri enim facere non licet quod quis sibi fieri non vult. . . . At, his omnibus non obstantibus, si altera pars, monita iam et edocta de tali morbo existente in comparte, nihilominus consentiat, licebit eis matrimonium uti, et si nondum contraxerint, illud contrahere: scienti enim et volenti non fit iniuria." — Iorio, *loc. cit.*

time as the disease is rendered incommunicable.[131] Therefore, if one afflicted with such a disease desires to marry, he may avoid violating the natural law in one of two ways: either by informing the other party of the presence of the disease, or by postponing marriage until the disease has been rendered incommunicable.[132]

In the meantime, until one of these two alternatives has been verified, the presence of a communicable social disease which is unknown to the other party renders marriage illicit. Inasmuch as it is thus an obstacle to marriage, the ascertainment that no such disease is present should form a part of the prenuptial investigation.[133] The responsibility of making this a part of the prenuptial investigation rests upon the local ordinary.[134] For he is the one charged with the duty of formulating the particular norms of the prenuptial investigation.[135]

Moreover, whenever this prenuptial investigation reveals the presence of a communicable social disease which is unknown to the other party, it is the duty of the local ordinary, in order to prevent a grave injustice to the innocent consort and to avoid a serious violation of the natural law, to prohibit the marriage until the other party has been informed of the presence of the disease, or until the disease itself has been rendered incommunicable. The authority to impose this matrimonial ban is granted to the local ordinary by canon 1039, §1.

---

131. "Ex iure naturae hoc matrimonium, utpote gravis iniuria, est graviter illicitum, usque dum morbus ita sanatus fuerit ut periculum eum comparti importandi remotum fuerit." — Payen, *loc. cit.*

132. "Nisi prius syphilide, horrendo et valde contagioso morbo, recreatus fuerit, aut saltem pars sana, quam intendit ducere, sciens ac volens, consenserit." — Payen, *ibid.*, n. 540.

133. S. C. de Sacr., instr., 29 iun. 1941: "Neminem latet gravem in sacramentum iniuriam committere, ideoque nec levi commaculari crimine, nupturientes qui ad matrimonium accedant haud servatis praeceptis ab Ecclesia naviter statutis ut christianae nuptiae licite . . . ineantur." — *AAS*, XXXIII (1941), 297; Bouscaren, *op. cit.*, II, 253.

134. "Ad rem Ecclesia onus commisit animarum praesulibus impertiendi parochis sibi subiectis idoneas normas pro investigationibus sedulo et opportuno tempore peragendis, ne matrimonio ineundo aliquid obstet." — *Ibid.*, p. 298.

135. "Ordinarii loci est peculiares normas pro huiusmodi parochi investigatione dare." — Canon 1020, §3.

CHAPTER VI

PENALTIES WHICH MAY BE ANNEXED TO A MATRIMONIAL BAN

Local ordinaries are empowered by the Code to impose in particular cases and for a just cause a matrimonial ban.[1] This matrimonial ban is a species of personal precept.[2] As such, it can be fortified with specific penalties to be incurred in the event that the prohibition is violated. For, in general, the Code grants to those capable of making laws or of imposing precepts the power to fortify these with penalties.[3]

This is true in the case of all local ordinaries with the exception of the vicar general. He has need of a special mandate in order that he may impose penalties,[4] and without this special mandate any attempt which he might make to impose such penalties would be invalid.[5]

Therefore, all local ordinaries with the exception of the vicar general may annex penalties to the matrimonial ban in order to urge its observance. The vicar general may annex such penalties only if he has received a special mandate empowering him to do so. Furthermore, without such a special mandate the vicar general cannot even apply a penalty which the bishop may have added to his matrimonial ban as a *ferendae sententiae* penalty. Thus, without a special mandate the vicar general can neither inflict nor apply penalties for the non-observance of a matrimonial ban.[6]

In forbidding the marriage, the local ordinary may impose the precept on the parties concerned and also on the pastor if he deems it

---

1. Canon 1039, §1.
2. Cf. pages 62-64 of this work.
3. "Qui pollent potestate leges ferendi vel praecepta imponendi, possunt quoque legi vel praecepto poenas adnectere." — Canon 2220, §1.
4. *Ibid.*, §2.
5. Coronata, *Institutiones*, IV, n. 1693.
6. Roberti, *De Delictis et Poenis*, Vol. I, Pars I, *de delictis in genere* (impressio altera emendata, Romae: Apud Custodiam Librariam Pontificii Instituti Utriusque Iuris, 1944), n. 56; Cappello, *De Censuris*, nn. 12 and 14; Chelodi-Ciprotti, *De Delictis et Poenis*, nn. 24 and 25; Coronata, *loc. cit.*

advisable.[7] The local ordinary (but not the vicar general without a special mandate) may likewise annex a penalty to this precept, both as regards the parties themselves and as regards the pastor.[8]

The penalty which he employs as a sanction for the matrimonial ban must be the threat of a punishment to be incurred upon a violation of the ban.[9] Although some canonists are of the opinion that the threatened punishment must be one which is clearly determined at the time it is threatened,[10] this conclusion does not seem to be warranted by the law of the Code. For the Code merely says: "... datur praeceptum, quo quid agere quidve evitare praeventus debeat, accurate indicetur, cum poenae comminatione in casu transgressionis."[11] Thus the Code seems to leave it to the judgment of the one threatening the penalty to decide whether he wishes to make the penalty a clearly determined one or to leave it indeterminate.

Likewise the Instruction *Cum magnopere* of June 11, 1880, did not seem to demand that the punishment be clearly determined. For this Instruction merely stated: "... ut delinquenti analogum iniungatur praeceptum, in quo declaretur quid eidem agendum aut omittendum sit, cum respondentis poenae ecclesiasticae comminatione, quam incurret in casu transgressionis."[12] The words *"cum respondentis poenae ecclesiasticae comminatione"* seem merely to indicate the threat of a "fitting" or "proportionate" ecclesiastical penalty.

Therefore, in view of the law as it is expressed in the Code, and in the absence of any clear indication to the contrary, it seems that when invoking a sanction for the matrimonial ban, the local ordinary (but not the vicar general without a special mandate) must indeed

---

7. Payen, *De Matrimonio,* I, n. 587.

8. Canon 2220, §1.

9. Canon 2310.

10. Cf. Coronata, *Institutiones,* IV, n. 1846; Ayrinhac-Lydon, *Penal Legislation in the New Code of Canon Law* (New York-Boston-Cincinnati-Chicago-San Francisco: Benziger Bros., 1936), n. 182; Esswein, *The Extrajudicial Coercive Powers of Ecclesiastical Superiors,* The Catholic University of America Canon Law Studies, n. 127 (Washington, D. C.: The Catholic University of America Press, 1941), p. 106.

11. Canon 2310.

12. Art. VII, *Fontes,* n. 2005.

threaten a proportionate punishment, but may either make it determinate or leave it indeterminate according to his prudent judgment in view of the circumstances of the individual case.[13] For in many cases it would be very difficult, if not impossible, to estimate accurately the scandal which would be caused or the harm which would ensue from the violation of the matrimonial ban, and so it would be equally difficult, if not impossible, to determine beforehand what would constitute a proportionate punishment.[14]

The Code does not mention specifically which penalties may be imposed. Consequently, the local ordinary (but not the vicar general without a special mandate) may impose any penalty which he judges to be proportionate to the gravity of the violation of the matrimonial ban in the particular case. Moreover, these penalties may be either censures or vindictive penalties,[15] and may be established either as *latae* or *ferendae sententiae* punishments.[16]

As to the method of infliction, canon 1933, §4, states that the penalties of canonical penance, penal remedy, excommunication, suspension, and interdict may be inflicted after the manner of a precept without any judicial procedure.[17] Therefore, the local ordinary (but not the vicar general without a special mandate) may apply or declare any of the penalties mentioned in this canon in an extrajudicial manner

---

13. "... cum poenae comminatione in casu transgressionis." —Canon 2310.

14. Canon 2218, §1.

15. Canon 2216.

16. Canon 2217, §1, 2°.

17. "Poenitentia, remedium poenale, excommunicatio, suspensio, interdictum, dummodo delictum certum sit, infligi possunt etiam per modum praecepti extra iudicium." — Canon 1933, §4. There have been various interpretations as to the meaning of this canon. Some maintain that the enumeration in this canon is all-inclusive, while there are others who maintain that canon 1933, §4, does not purport to present a complete list and therefore allows the infliction of other penalties after the manner of a precept as well. For a thorough discussion of this problem cf. Esswein, *op. cit.*, pp. 110-114. "The conclusion that only those penalties which are mentioned in canon 1933, §4, may be inflicted and applied *per modum praecepti*, and then only when they are enacted as the result of a precept, seems fully recommended, since among the various opinions it reflects the closest conformity to, and the most intimate harmony with, the spirit which actuates all of the Church's legislation." —*Ibid.*, p. 114.

per modum praecepti; other penalties should be applied or declared *per processum iudicialem.*[18] The excommunication is necessarily a censure, but the suspension and interdict may be established either as censures or as vindictive penalties.[19]

If the matrimonial ban has been imposed with the threat of a *determined* penalty, no further admonition is required if the ban is violated. For if the threatened penalty is a *latae sententiae* penalty, it takes effect immediately;[20] if it is a *ferendae sententiae* penalty, it may be inflicted immediately.[21] If, however, the *ferendae sententiae* penalty is a censure and the delinquent recedes from his contumacy before its infliction, it can no longer be inflicted.[22] On the other hand, since this restriction refers only to censures, a vindictive penalty could still be inflicted.[23]

If the matrimonial ban has been imposed with the threat of an *indeterminate* penalty, the penalty will necessarily be of a *ferendae sententiae* character.[24] If the penalty is vindictive, no further admonition is required subsequent to the violation of the ban, and the penalty

---

18. Canon 2225 in conjunction with canon 1933, §4.

19. Canon 2255, §2.

20. Canons 2217, §1, 2°; 2232, §1; 2242, §2. "Monitio *a iure* obtinet in poenis latae sententiae. Eadem censetur contineri in legi vel praecepto quo aliquid iubetur vel vetatur, quia lex interpellat pro homine. Ideo ad incurrendam censuram sufficit transgressio legis vel praecepti, cui censura adnexa est. In hoc casu contumacia consistit in formali spretu legis vel praecepti; eademque dicitur *contumacia interpretativa.*" — Roberti, *op. cit.*, n. 283.

21. Canon 2233; *Pontificia Commissio ad Codicis Canones authentice Interpretandos,* 14 iul. 1922: "Utrum, ad normam can. 2233, §2, ob violationem praecepti peculiaris, quod communitum erat censura ferendae sententiae, statim post delictum comprabatum censura infligi possit; an vero praemittenda sit nova monitio." Resp: Affirmative ad lam partem; negative as 2am. — *AAS,* XIV (1922), 530; Bouscaren, *The Canon Law Digest,* I, 845.

22. "... contumacia persistente, censura infligi potest." — Canon 2233, §2. Cf. Coronata, *Institutiones,* IV, n. 1724.

23. "Aliter dicendum esset si ageretur de poena vindicativa; non enim in hoc casu poenitentia delicti vel remotio effectuum facere possunt ut quis poenam effugiat." — Roberti, *op. cit.*, n. 282 in nota.

24. "Poena indeterminata latae sententiae repugnat." — Coronata, *Institutiones,* IV, n. 1690.

can be inflicted immediately.[25] However, if the penalty is a censure, the person must be reprimanded and warned to desist from contumacy subsequent to the violation of the ban before the penalty can be inflicted. Moreover, if in the prudent judgment of the ordinary it seems fitting, a suitable time should be allowed for the delinquent to comply. It is only if the contumacy continues after this warning that the censure can be inflicted.[26]

It will be left to the prudent judgment of the local ordinary (but not the vicar general without a special mandate) to determine in each individual case which of these penalties is to be imposed and under what form it will prove to be most effective.

---

25. ". . . neque necessaria est praevia monitio canonica, si agatur de infligenda poena vindicativa, eo quod haec non fertur ad frangendam rei contumaciam." — Beste, *Introductio in Codicem*, p. 918.

26. Canons 2233, §2; 2242, §2. "Haec correptio et monitio consistit in intimatione legitima facta, qua superior subdito delinquenti comminatur, ipsum censura aliqua specifica et determinata mulctatum iri, nisi resipiscat et pareat. . . . Ratio est, quia censura non infligitur nisi in contumacem; atqui de tali actuali contumacia in censuris ferendae sententiae non constat nisi praecesserit monitio ad tramitem can. 2242, §2. Aliter res se habet in censuris latae sententiae, nam ibi ipsa lex vel praeceptum illam monitionem canonicam continet." — Beste, *loc. cit.*

CONCLUSIONS

Prior to the Code:

1. The prohibition of the Church with reference to the contracting of a marriage existed in general as an impedient impediment.

2. Only the Roman Pontiff was competent to add to his prohibition an invalidating decree.

3. The bishop was empowered to prohibit a marriage, but he lacked the power of appending to his prohibition an invalidating clause. However, it was within his power to impose very severe penalties for the violation of his prohibition.

4. Although the pastor was unable to adjudicate a matrimonial cause, it was nevertheless within his power to prohibit a marriage extrajudicially until the competent judge had rendered a judicial decision.

5. The parties concerned were to be temporarily separated as a punishment for their violation of the ecclesiastical prohibition of their marriage. This penalty was to be commuted to some other form of punishment whenever there was danger of incontinence on the part of the spouses concerned.

6. The children of a marriage which had been contracted in violation of an ecclesiastical prohibition and was subsequently found to be invalid were to be considered illegitimate, notwithstanding the ignorance of the parents in regard to the presence of the diriment impediment.

The Law of the Code:

7. A marriage contracted in violation of the prohibition of the local ordinary is illicit but not invalid.

8. The imposition of a matrimonial ban by the local ordinary is a species of personal precept. As such, it is governed by the prescriptions of canon 24 as well as those of canon 1039, §1.

9. A matrimonial ban which has been imposed through a legal document can be fortified with specific penalties to be incurred in the event that the prohibition is violated.

10. The power of the local ordinary to impose a matrimonial ban is a species of ordinary power; as such it can be delegated according to the prescription of canon 199, §1.

11. The powers of the vicar general are not so extensive in regard to the matrimonial ban as are those of the local bishop. For the vicar general is unable to annex penalties to a matrimonial ban and cannot punish the violation of his prohibition of a particular marriage with the infliction of a penalty as long as he has not received a special mandate empowering him to do so.

12. Some of the causes which warrant the imposition of a matrimonial ban by the local ordinary are: the reasonable dissent of the parents of minors; a prudent doubt concerning the freedom of the parties to contract marriage; the emergence of scandal; a sinful intention to abuse the marital right; and the presence of a communicable social disease which is unknown to the other party.

13. The local ordinary (but not the vicar general without a special mandate) may annex a penalty to his matrimonial ban, both as regards the parties themselves and as regards the pastor. In so doing, he must threaten a proportionate punishment, but he may either make it determinate or leave it indeterminate according to his prudent judgment in view of the circumstances of the individual case.

BIBLIOGRAPHY

Sources

Acta Apostolicae Sedis, Commentarium Officiale, Romae, 1909- .

Acta et Decreta Concilii Provincialis Portlandensis in Oregon Quarti, 10 sept. 1932.

Acta Sanctae Sedis, 41 vols., Romae, 1865-1908.

Bouscaren, T. Lincoln, *The Canon Law Digest,* 2 vols. and supplement through 1948, Milwaukee: Bruce, 1934, 1943, 1949.

Bruns, H., *Canones Apostolorum et Conciliorum Saeculorum IV-VII,* 2 vols., Berolini, 1839.

Canones et Decreta Concilii Tridentini, ex Editione Romana a. 1834 Repetiti, Accedunt S. Cong. Card. Conc. Trid. Interpretum Declarationes ac Resolutiones ex Ipso Resolutionum Thesauro, et Constitutiones Pontificiae Recentiores ad Ius Commune Spectantes, Neapoli, 1859.

Codex Iuris Canonici Pii X Pontificis Maximi iussu digestus Benedicti Papae XV Auctoritate promulgatus, praefatione, fontium annotatione et indice analytico-alphabetico ab Emo Petro Card. Gasparri Auctus, Romae: Typis Polyglottis Vaticanis, 1917.

Codicis Iuris Canonici Fontes, cura Emi Petri Card. Gasparri, editi, 9 vols., Romae (postea Civitate Vaticana): Typis Polyglottis Vaticanis, 1923-1939 (Vols. VII, VIII, et IX, ed. cura et studio Emi Iustiniani Card. Serédi).

Corpus Iuris Canonici, ed. Lipsiensis 2, post Aemilii Ludovici Richteri curas . . . instruxit Aemilius Friedberg, 2 vols., Lipsiae: Tauchnitz, 1879-1881; ed. anastatice repetita, 1928.

Decretales D. Gregorii Papae IX, suae integritati, una cum glossis restitutae, Romae, 1582.

Decretum Gratiani, emendatum et notationibus illustratum, una cum glossis, 2 vols., Romae, 1582.

Hardouin, Jean, *Acta Conciliorum et Epistolae Decretales ac Constitutiones Summorum Pontificum,* 12 vols., Parisiis, 1714-1715.

Jaffé, Philippus, *Regesta Pontificum Romanorum ab condita Ecclesia ad annum post Christum natum MCXCVIII,* 2. ed., correctam et auctam auspiciis Gulielmi Wattenbach, curaverunt S. Loewenfeld, F. Kaltenbrunner, P. Ewald, 2 toms. in 1 vol., Lipsiae: Veit, et Comp., 1885-1888.

Liber Sextus Decretalium D. Bonifatii Papae VIII, suae integretati una cum Clementinis et Extravagantibus, earumque Glossis restitutus, Romae, 1582.

Magnum Bullarium Romanum, seu Eiusdem Continuatio, 19 vols., Luxemburgi, 1727-1758.

Mansi, J. D., *Sacrorum Conciliorum Nova et Amplissima Collectio,* 53 vols. in 60, Paris-Leipzig-Arnhem, 1901-1927.

Monumenta Germaniae Historica, 188 vols., incomplete, Hanoverae, 1826- , *Epistolae,* Tom. VII, Pars Prior, *Johannis VIII Papae Registrum,* ed. Ericus Caspar, Berolini: apud Weidmannos, 1912.

Potthast, Augustus, *Regesta Pontificum Romanorum inde ab anno post Christum natum MCXCVIII ad annum MCCCIV,* 2 vols., Berolini, 1874-1875.

Schroeder, H. J., *Canons and Decrees of the Council of Trent: Original Text with English Translation,* St. Louis: B. Herder Book Co., 1941.

Synodus Archidioecesis Sancti Francisci Secunda, 14 oct. 1936, San Francisco: Monitor Publishing Co., 1936.

Synodus Dioecesana Fargensis Prima, 29-30 sept. 1941, Milwauchiae: Ex Typographia Bruce, 1941.

Thesaurus Resolutionum Sacrae Congregationis Concilii, 167 vols., Romae, 1718-1908.

Reference Works

Aertnys, J.-Damen, C., *Theologia Moralis,* 14. ed., 2 vols., Romae: Marietti, 1944.

Alford, Culver Bernard, *Jus Matrimoniale Comparatum,* New York: P. J. Kenedy and Sons, 1938.

Aquinas, St. Thomas, *Opera Omnia,* ad Fidem Optimarum Editionum, 22 vols., Parmae: Typis Petri Fiaccadori, 1852-1868.

———, *Opera Omnia,* Vol. XIII, *De Malo,* Parisiis, 1875.

———, *Summa Theologica,* 6 vols., Taurini: Marietti, 1932.

Ayrinhac, H. A.-Lydon, P. J., *Marriage Legislation in the New Code of Canon Law,* 2. ed., New York: Benziger Bros., 1943.

———, *Penal Legislation in the New Code of Canon Law,* New York: Benziger Bros., 1936.

Bandinelli, Rolandus, *Die Summa Magistri Rolandi,* herausgegeben von Dr. Friederich Thaner, Innsbruck, 1874.

Barbosa, A., *Collectanea Doctorum tam Veterum quam Recentiorum in Ius Pontificium Universum,* 5 vols., Lugduni, 1656.

———, *Pastoralis Solicitudinis sive De Officio et Potestate Episcopi,* Pars III, Lugduni, 1556.

Bastnagel, Clement V., *The Appointment of Parochial Adjutants and Assistants,* The Catholic University of America Canon Law Studies, n. 58, Washington, D. C.: The Catholic University of America, 1930.

Benedictus XIV, *De Synodo Dioecesana,* 4 vols., Mechliniae, 1842.

Bernardus Papiensis, *Summa Decretalium,* ed. E. Laspeyres, Ratisbonae, 1860.

Beste, U., *Introductio in Codicem,* 3. ed., Collegeville, Minn.: St. John's Abbey Press, 1946.

Blat, A., *Commentarium Textus Codicis Iuris Canonici,* 5 vols. in 6, Romae: Collegio "Angelico"; Vol. III, 2. ed., 1924; Vol. VI, *De Delictis et Poenis,* 1924.

Böckhn, Placidus, *Commentarius in Ius Canonicum Universum,* 3 vols., Salisburgi, et invenitur Parisiis, 1776.

Bouscaren, T. L.-Ellis, A. C., *Canon Law,* Milwaukee: The Bruce Publishing Co., 1948.

Bucceroni, G., *Institutiones Theologiae Moralis,* Vol. I, 4. ed., Romae, 1900.

Cappello, Felix M., *Summa Iuris Canonici in Usum Scholarum,* 3 vols., Vol. I, 4. ed., 1945, Romae: Apud Aedes Universitatis Gregorianae.

———, *Tractatus Canonico-Moralis de Censuris iuxta Codicem Iuris Canonici,* ed. altera, Taurini: Marietti, 1925.

———, *Tractatus Canonico-Moralis de Sacramentis,* 5 vols., Romae: Marietti; Vol. V, *De Matrimonio,* 5. ed., 1947.

Cerato, P., *Matrimonium a Codice I. C. integre Desumptum,* 4. ed., Patavii: Typis Seminarii Patavini, 1927.

Chelodi, Ioannes, *Ius Canonicum de Personis,* 3. ed., Trento: Libreria Moderna Editrice, 1942.

———, *Ius de Personis iuxta Codicem Iuris Canonici,* Tridenti: Libr. Edit. Tridentum, 1927.

———, *Ius Poenale et Ordo Procedendi in Iudiciis Criminalibus iuxta Codicem Iuris Canonici,* Tridenti: Libr. Edit. Tridentum, 1925.

Chelodi, Ioannes,-Ciprotti, Pio, *Ius Canonicum de Delictis et Poenis et de Iudiciis Criminalibus,* 5. ed., Trento: Libreria Moderna Editrice, 1943.

Chrétien, P., *De Matrimonio Praelectiones,* 2. ed., Metis: Typis Imprimierie du Journal "Le Lorrain," 1937.

Cicognani, Amleto, *Canon Law,* second revised ed., Westminster, Maryland: Newman Bookshop, 1946.

Claeys Bouuaert, F. et Simenon, G., *Manuale Iuris Canonici ad usum Seminariorum,* 3 vols., Gandae et Leodii: Apud Auctores in Seminariis Gandavensi et Leodiensi, Vol. II, 1931.

Cocchi, Guidus, *Commentarium in Codicem Iuris Canonici ad Usum Scholarum,* 8 vols., Vol. I, ed. V recognita, Taurini: Marietti, 1938.

Coronata, Matthaeus, Conte a, *Institutiones Iuris Canonici ad Usum Utriusque Cleri et Scholarum,* 2. ed., 5 vols., Taurini: Marietti, 1939-1947; Vol. I, 1939; Vol. III, 1941; Vol. IV, 1945.

———, *Institutiones Iuris Canonici ad usum utriusque cleri et scholarum, De Sacramentis Tractatus Canonicus,* 3 vols., Taurini, Romae: Marietti, 1943-1946; Vol. III, *De Matrimonio,* 1946.

Davis, H., *Moral and Pastoral Theology,* 4. ed., revised and enlarged, 4 vols., New York: Sheed and Ward, 1943.

De Smet, A., *Tractatus Theologico-Canonicus de Sponsalibus et Matrimonio,* ed. quarta inde a Codice altera, Brugis: Car. Beyaert, 1927.

Durantis, Gulielmus, *Speculum Judiciale,* Venetiis, 1577.

Esswein, Anthony A., *The Extrajudicial Coercive Powers of Ecclesiastical Superiors,* The Catholic University of America Canon Law Studies, n. 127, Washington, D. C.: The Catholic University of America Press, 1941.

Fagnanus, P., *Commentaria in Quinque Libros Decretalium,* 4 vols., Venetiis, 1696.

Gasparri, Petrus, *Tractatus Canonicus de Matrimonio,* 2 vols., Parisiis, 1891.

———, *Tractatus Canonicus de Matrimonio,* ed. nova ad mentem Codicis I. C., 2 vols., Romae: Typis Polyglottis Vat., 1932.

Gonzalez-Tellez, Emmanuel, *Commentaria Perpetua in Singulos Textus Quinque Librorum Decretalium Gregorii IX,* 5 vols., Lugduni, 1673.

Gougnard, Armandus, *Tractatus de Matrimonio,* 7. ed., Mechliniae: H. Dessain, 1931.

Gury, P.-Tummolo, R.-Iorio, T., *Compendium Theologiae Moralis,* 5. ed., 2 vols., Neapoli: M. D'Auria, 1934-1935.

Heylen, V., *Tractatus de Matrimonio,* 9. ed., Mechliniae: H. Dessain, 1945.

Hostiensis (Henricus Card. de Segusio), *In Quinque Libros Decretalium Commentaria,* 5 vols. in 3, Venetiis, 1581.

———, *Summa Aurea,* Venetiis, 1586.

Iorio, T., *Theologia Moralis,* 3 vols., Neapoli: M. D'Auria, 1946-1947.

Kearney, Raymond A., *The Principles of Delegation*, The Catholic University of America Canon Law Studies, n. 55, Washington, D. C.: The Catholic University of America, 1929.

Maroto, P., *Institutiones Iuris Canonici ad Normam Novi Codicis*, 2 vols., Vol. I, 3. ed., Romae, 1921.

Migne, J. P., *Patrologiae Cursus Completus, Series Graeca*, 161 vols., Parisiis, 1857-1866.

———, *Patrologiae Cursus Completus, Series Latina*, 221 vols., Parisiis, 1844-1864.

Navarrus (Martinus de Azpilcueta), *Consiliorum Seu Responsorum Tomus Alter*, Venetiis, 1621.

Neuberger, Nicholas J., *Canon 6 or the Relation of the Codex Iuris Canonici to the Preceding Legislation*, The Catholic University of America Canon Law Studies, n. 44, Washington, D. C.: The Catholic University of America, 1927.

Noldin, H.-Schmitt, A., *Summa Theologiae Moralis*, 27. ed., 3 vols., Oeniponte-Lipsiae: Sumptibus et Typis F. Rauch, 1940-1941.

———, *De Sexto Praecepto et De Usu Matrimonii*, 31. ed., Oeniponte-Lipsiae: Sumptibus et Typis F. Rauch, 1940.

O'Donnell, Cletus F., *The Marriage of Minors*, The Catholic University of America Canon Law Studies, n. 221, Washington, D. C.: The Catholic University of America Press, 1945.

Panormitanus Abbas (Nicholaus de Tudeschis), *Omnia Quae Extant Commentaria*, 8 vols., Venetiis, 1588.

Payen, G., *De Matrimonio in Missionibus ac Potissimum in Sinis Tractatus Practicus*, ed. altera, 3 vols., Zi-ka-wei: in Typographia T'ou-sè-wè, 1935-1936.

Pirhing, Ernricus, *Ius Canonicum in Quinque Libros Decretalium Distributum Nova Methodo Explicatum*, ed. novissima, 5 vols. in 4, Dilingae, 1674-1678; Vol. I, 1674.

Pontius, B., *De Sacramento Matrimonii Tractatus*, Venetiis, 1756.

Prierias, Sylvester, *Summa Sylvestrina, Quae Summa Summorum merito Nuncupatur*, 2 vols., Venetiis, 1601.

Prümmer, Dominicus M., *Manuale Theologiae Moralis secundum Principia S. Thomae Aquinatis*, 10. ed., 3 vols., Barcelona: Editorial Herder, 1946.

Quasten, Johannes-Plumpe, Joseph, *The Works of the Fathers in Translation*, incomplete, Westminster, Maryland: The Newman Bookshop, 1946- ; Vol. I, *The Epistles of St. Clement of Rome, and St. Ignatius of Antioch* (newly translated and annotated by James A. Kleist, S. J.), 1946.

Raymundus de Pennafort, Saint, *Summa,* Veronae, 1744.

Regatillo, Eduardus F., *Institutiones Iuris Canonici,* 2. ed., 2 vols., Santander: Sal Terrae, 1946.

Reiffenstuel, Anacletus, *Ius Canonicum Universum,* 5 vols. in 6, Romae, 1831-1834.

———, *Ius Canonicum Universum,* 5 vols. in 7, Parisiis, 1864-1870.

Roberti, F., *De Delictis et Poenis,* Vol. I, Impressio altera emendata, Romae: Apud Custodiam Librariam Pontificii Instituti Utriusque Iuris, 1944.

———, *De Processibus,* 2 vols., Romae: Apud Aedes Facultatis Iuridicae ad S. Apollinaris, 1926.

Romani, S., *Institutiones Iuris Canonici,* 2 vols. in 3, Romae: Editrice "Iustitia," 1941-1945.

Rossi, Joseph, *De Matrimonii Celebratione iuxta Codicem Iuris Canonici,* Romae: Fridericus Pustet, 1924.

Rupprecht, Theodorus, *Notae Historicae in Universum Ius Canonicum,* Venetiis, 1764.

Salucci, R., *Il Diritto Penale Secondo il Codice di Diritto Canonico,* 2 vols. in 1, Subiaco, 1926-1930.

Sanchez, Thomas, *De Sancti Matrimonii Sacramento Disputationum Tomi Tres,* Antverpiae, 1626.

Sandeus, Felinus, *Commentaria in Quinque Libros Decretalium,* 5 vols. in 3, Venetiis, 1570.

Santi, Franciscus, *Praelectiones Iuris Canonici,* 5 vols. in 2, Ratisbonae, Neo Eboraci, et Cincinnati, 1886.

Schmalzgrueber, F., *Ius Ecclesiasticum Universum,* 5 vols. in 12, Romae, 1843-1845.

Schmier, F., *Jurisprudentia Canonico-Civilis seu Ius Canonicum Universum,* 2 vols., Venetiis, 1754.

Stutz, U., *Der Geist des Codex iuris canonici, Kirchenrechtliche Abhandlungen,* 92. und 93. Heft, Stuttgart: Verlag von Ferdinand Enke, 1918.

Van Hove, A., *Commentarium Lovaniense in Codicem Iuris Canonici,* 5 tomes, Mechliniae-Romae: H. Dessain, 1928-1939. Vol. I, *Prolegomena,* 2. ed., 1945; Vol. II, *De Legibus Ecclesiasticis,* 1930.

Vermeersch, A.-Creusen, J., *Epitome Iuris Canonici,* 3 vols., Vol. I, 6. ed., 1937; Vol II, 6. ed., 1940; Vol. III, 6. ed., 1946, Mechliniae-Romae: H. Dessain.

Vlaming, Th. M., *Praelectiones Iuris Canonici ad Normam Codicis Iuris Canonici,* 3. ed., 2 vols., Bussum in Hollandia: Sumptibus Societatis Editricis Anonymae olim Paulus Brand, 1919-1921.

Wernz, F. X., *Ius Decretalium,* 6 vols., Vol. II, Romae, 1899; Vol. IV, *Ius Matrimoniale,* Romae, 1904.

Wernz, F. X.-Vidal, P., *Ius Canonicum ad Codicem Normam Exactum,* 7 vols. in 8, Vol. I, 1938; Vol. II, 3. ed., a P. Aguirre recognita, 1943; Vol. V, *Ius Matrimoniale,* 3. ed., a P. Aguirre recognita, 1946, Romae: Apud Aedes Universitatis Gregorianae.

Woywod, S., *A Practical Commentary on the Code of Canon Law,* 2. ed., New York: Wagner, 1926.

Articles

Bastnagel, C., "Doubtful Competence of the Vicar General," *The Jurist,* VIII (1948), 213-219.

Clarke, C. W., "The Conquest of Venereal Disease," *Hygeia,* XXVII (1949), 164-165, 201.

Connell, F. J., "May the State Forbid Marriage Because of a Social Disease?" *The Ecclesiastical Review,* XCIX (1938), 507-518.

Roelker, E., "The Vicar General and the Special Mandate," *The Jurist,* II (1942), 346-362.

———, "The Power to Enact Invalidating Laws," *The Jurist,* III (1943), 231-257.

Toso, A., "Summa de Officio et Potestate Vicarii Generalis," *Jus Pontificium,* VII (1927), 138-146.

Periodicals

American Ecclesiastical Review, The, Vols. I-XXXII, Philadelphia, 1889-1905; from 1905: *The Ecclesiastical Review,* Vols. XXXIII-CIX, Philadelphia, 1905-1943; from 1944: *The American Ecclesiastical Review,* Washington, D. C., Vol. CX, 1944- .

Hygeia, Chicago, Ill., 1923- .

Jurist, The, Washington, D. C., 1941- .

Jus Pontificium, Romae, 1921-1940.

ABBREVIATIONS

AAS — *Acta Apostolicae Sedis.*

ASS — *Acta Sanctae Sedis.*

Bruns — *Canones Apostolorum et Conciliorum Saeculorum IV-VII.*

C. — Causa.

c. — canon or caput.

D. — Distinctio.

Fontes — *Codicis Iuris Canonici Fontes.*

Hardouin — *Acta Conciliorum, etc.*

Jaffé — *Regesta Pontificum Romanorum, etc.*

Mansi — *Sacrorum Conciliorum Nova et Amplissima Collectio.*

MGH — *Monumenta Germaniae Historica.*

MPG — Migne, *Patrologiae Cursus Completus, Series Graeca.*

MPL — Migne, *Patrologiae Cursus Completus, Series Latina.*

Potthast — *Regesta Pontificum Romanorum, etc.*

S. C. C. — *Sacra Congregatio Concilii.*

S. C. de Sacr. — *Sacra Congregatio de Disciplina Sacramentorum.*

BIOGRAPHICAL NOTE

John M. Waterhouse was born March 30, 1919, at Salt Lake City, Utah. Shortly thereafter he moved with his parents to Saranac Lake, New York. He received his grammar school and high school education in St. Bernard's Parochial School and the Saranac Lake High School at Saranac Lake. He attended Lake Forest University, Lake Forest, Illinois. Later he entered Wadhams Hall Seminary in Ogdensburg, New York, and there made his philosophical studies. His theological studies he made at St. Bernard's Seminary in Rochester, New York. He was ordained to the priesthood on March 17, 1945, by His Excellency, Bryan J. McEntegart, Bishop of Ogdensburg. In the fall of 1947 he entered upon a course of studies in the School of Canon Law at The Catholic University of America, Washington, D. C., where he received the Baccalaureate degree in Canon Law in June, 1948, and the Licentiate degree in Canon Law in June, 1949.

ALPHABETICAL INDEX

CANON LAW STUDIES*

306. Waters, Rev. Joseph L., S. S. J., J. C. L., The Probation in Societies of Quasi-Religious.

307. Regan, Rev. Michael J., J. C. L., Canon 16.

308. Byrne, Rev. Harry J., J. C. L., Investment of Church Funds.

309. Gallagher, Rev. Thomas V., J. C. L., The Rejection of Judicial Witnesses and Testimony.

310. Chatham, Rev. Josiah G., Ph. D., S. T. L., J. C. L., Force and Fear as Invalidating Marriage: The Element of Injustice.

311. Brown, Rev. James Victor, O. R. S. A., J. C. L., The Invalidating Effects of Force, Fear, and Fraud upon the Canonical Novitiate.

312. Duerr, Rev. Charles J., B. A., J. C. L., The Judicial Notary.

313. Gonzalez, Rev. Francisco J., O. S. A., J. C. L., De Parocho Religioso Eiusque Superiore Locali.

314. Hannon, Rev. James J., J. C. L., Holy Viaticum.

315. Sadlowski, Rev. Edwin L., J. C. L., The Sacred Furnishings of Churches.

316. Sego, Rev. Arthur A., J. C. L., Dispensation from the Interpellations.

317. Waterhouse, Rev. John M., J. C. L., The Power of the Local Ordinary to Impose a Matrimonial Ban.

318. Frein, Rev. Eugene B., J. C. L., The Discretionary Power of the Defender of the Matrimonial Bond.

319. Carton, Rev. George A., J. C. L., The Time Factor in the Gaining of Indulgences.

320. Walsh, Rev. John J., C. S. Sp., J. C. L., The Jurisdiction of the Interritual Confessor in the United States and Canada.

321. Unterkoefler, Rev. Ernest L., S. T. L., J. C. L., The Presiding Judge in Matrimonial Causes of First Instance.

*A complete list of the available numbers in the series will be found in earlier studies. Send orders to: The Catholic University of America Press, 620 Michigan Ave., N. E., Washington 17, D. C.

www.ingramcontent.com/pod-product-compliance
Lightning Source LLC
LaVergne TN
LVHW050211080826
844660LV00012B/393

9780813224923